THE POWER TO CHOOSE

Finding Calm and Connection
in a Complex World

ROBBIE SWALE

Winds of Trust Publications

Copyright © 2025 Robbie Swale

First published 2025 by Winds of Trust Publications
First edition, 2025

The right of Robbie Swale to be identified as the author
of this work has been asserted by him in accordance with the
Copyright, Designs and Patents Act 1988.

All rights reserved. No part of this publication may be reproduced,
stored in a retrieval system, or transmitted in any other form or by
any means, electronic, mechanical, photocopying, recording or otherwise, without
the prior permission of the publisher.

This book is for educational and informational purposes.
It's about offering ideas, stories, and practices that you can explore
in your own life and work. It isn't medical, psychological, or legal advice.
If you're experiencing significant distress or health concerns, please
seek support from a qualified professional.

ISBN 978-1-915266-04-0
www.robbieswale.com

CONTENTS

About the Author — 5
Also by Robbie Swale — 6
Praise — 7
Introduction — 11
How to Use This Book — 24

Part One — 27

Chapter One:
You Can Choose — 29

Chapter Two:
What If Everyone Is Doing Their Best? — 57

Chapter Three:
Curiosity Is the Antidote to Contraction — 91

Part Two — 119

Chapter Four:
No One Can Compete with You at Being You — 121

Chapter Five:
Relationships of Possibility — 149

Conclusion — 193
Acknowledgements — 199
Endnotes — 207

ABOUT THE AUTHOR

Robbie Swale is a leadership coach, podcaster and author whose work focuses on leading in complexity, meaningful productivity and the craft of coaching.

He works one-to-one with leaders and entrepreneurs, and with teams, on how to get the things that *really matter* done. Alongside his work with leaders who contract him directly, he has run leadership development interventions for organisations including Deutsche Bank, 64 Million Artists, Moonpig and the University of Edinburgh.

He is the creator of *The Meaningful Productivity Blueprint* (available from www.robbieswale.com for free), the host of *The 12-Minute Method Podcast* and the author of The 12-Minute Method series of books about creativity and procrastination, including *How to Start When You're Stuck* and *How to Create the Conditions for Great Work*.

A firm believer in the power of coaching to tilt the world towards heaven and away from hell, Robbie supports the coaching industry as the founder of The Coach's Journey. He is the host of *The Coach's Journey Podcast* and the creator of *The Coaching Business Flywheel*.

Read more about Robbie's work, subscribe to his weekly 12-minute blog and more at www.robbieswale.com.

You can email Robbie at hello@robbieswale.com.

ALSO BY ROBBIE SWALE

The 12-Minute Method Series

How to Start (a book, business or creative project) When You're Stuck

How to Keep Going (with a book, business or creative project) When You Want to Give Up

How to Create the Conditions for Great Work

How to Share What You've Made

Available from Amazon, here, or from your favourite bookshop:

Other Notable Works

The Meaningful Productivity Blueprint
– available for free at www.robbieswale.com

An Introduction to The Coaching Business Flywheel
– available for free at www.thecoachsjourney.com

PRAISE

'Each time I talk with Robbie, he gives me a new thought to think about.'

— Robert Holden, Author, Authentic Success

'Robbie introduced me to my own potential and I am so grateful to have met him.'

— Shivangi Raghuvanshi, Lead Program Manager, Asia, Microsoft

'Whilst my workload is exactly the same, if not increased, I feel more in control of my time, my diary, my work, my life. Hardly a day goes by without me thinking of something that Robbie and I discussed.'

— Professor Leonie Taams, King's College London

'Robbie will push you as far as you are willing to go and encourage you into places you didn't know existed – go with it: you can only end up somewhere more truthful than before!'

— Alice Mayor, Founder, We Built This City

'Robbie has helped me to change the way I think about my business, from one of worry and scarcity to one of possibility and abundance; the anxieties of first-time entrepreneurship have been replaced by joy and hopeful anticipation.'

— Faisal Sheikh, Managing Director, Monmouth Capital

'Working with Robbie has had a transformational impact on my career direction and ambition.'

— Charlotte Bennett, Co-Artistic Director, Paines Plough

'Robbie helped me to find the blockers in my mind and get ready to change.'

— John Monks, Co-Founder, Curve

'Robbie is a true professional and a master of his craft. I feel very fortunate to have found him.'

— Ed Burke, Co-Founder, Hemisphere Travel Group

'My business has gone from strength to strength, as well as areas of my personal life, and I really think that I wouldn't be in the confident, successful place that I am now if it weren't for Robbie.'

— Kate Rees, Founder, Kate Rees Coaching

A Note on Client Stories

Confidentiality is very important in my work as a coach. In this book, when I tell a story about a client, details have been changed to preserve that confidentiality and sometimes several clients' experiences have been amalgamated. If the story felt specific to someone in particular, I have asked permission from that client and they have kindly given it. In each case, I hope the spirit of the experience and the insights available in it have been maintained.

INTRODUCTION

I didn't mean to write a book. The idea for it first came into my mind when Joel Monk, my coach at the time, asked me what I would be excited to share with him if we met up several months later. It turned out, somewhat as a surprise to me, that I would be excited to share that I had written a book. I hadn't thought about it seriously before that moment and I'm not sure where it came from, but, as we discussed it, the topic for this book emerged.

Several years earlier, I had faced what psychologist and author Robert Holden calls an 'involuntary stop.' The world moves so fast these days that many of us fail to notice what is happening to us, running along at breakneck pace without ever really checking whether or not we want to be going in that direction in the first place. If we are lucky, or wise, we sometimes make a voluntary stop, slowing down and taking perspective. For many of us, however, it takes some form of adversity to stop us in our tracks. For me, it was the end of a relationship that had lasted since I was at university, which, at the time, was almost my whole adult life. The break-up seemed to come from nowhere and it disrupted my past, present and future. The gift of it, which I began to see once the pain slowly died down, was that I started to look at things differently.

After that involuntary stop, I craved an understanding of myself and the world on a deeper level and, over the years that followed, the new ways I found of looking at the world seemed to make all the difference across my life. The purpose of the book, which emerged through my conversation with Joel, was to find the answer to the question: is this new way of looking at the world valid?

The ideas in this book have left me happier and more fulfilled than at any previous point in my life. I have increased the impact I make through my work and enjoy it more than ever before. I have a better and more fulfilling romantic relationship. I am more courageous and more skilful across my life. I feel better about myself – and life as a whole – than before.[1]

This shift has been transformational for me and that's what this book is about: sharing this way of looking at the world in the hope that you find it transformational, too.

Making an Impact

When I was in my early 20s, I wanted to be a professional actor. I was probably good enough, too. One year, I *almost* got into four of the United Kingdom's top five drama schools. I was in final rounds, on shortlists, on reserve lists. I didn't get a place, though, and, as I reflected over the next year, I realised that a career as an actor may not have fulfilled me.

Strangely, this realisation came to me when I watched *The West Wing*, one of my favourite TV shows, following the fictional President Bartlet and his senior staff. I say 'strangely' because up until that point in my life, it was seeing amazing pieces of television, film or theatre that inspired me most towards a career as an actor. But *The West Wing* helped me realise something different: yes, taking part in a piece of art as influential as that would be an amazing way to make an impact on the world, but not as amazing as working in the *actual* White House. I had more strengths than just my ability to act and, as I discovered the fickle nature of the acting world (I

Introduction

didn't get through a single audition in my applications to drama schools the following year), I realised that to be fulfilled, I needed to make sure I was having as big an impact as I could. That needed to be in the real world, and not as a character in a show: in the real world, I would have much more control over how I used my strengths, and my career wouldn't be ruled nearly as much by the whims of a casting director.

I shifted my focus and began a career as a leader in arts and culture. My next two jobs were managing and running arts centres, leading teams of staff and volunteers (while briefly thinking of myself as the Yorkshire art scene's answer to Josh Lyman, President Bartlet's bolshy but effective Deputy Chief of Staff).

Then came the break-up and, forced by that shock to stop and look at my life, I saw something about my work. Whilst I was using *more* of my strengths than I might have as an actor, I was tired. Exhausted, in fact. At times, I found myself anxious and stressed, worrying at weekends, unable to sleep. And somehow, I no longer wanted to end up in the arts jobs that had once felt like a dream to me.

I started to see that the contribution I was making in the arts wasn't fulfilling me and I began to be seduced by ideas like the one that I first heard from the Integral Coach, Brett Thomas: that there might be a sweet spot where our skills, what we enjoy and the way we want to contribute to the world all meet. I set off in search of that and, several years later, found myself working as a leadership coach.

That was the first gift of the involuntary stop: it gave me the space and perspective to take action in my life, to choose something different.

But that was only part of the gift. I also realised that I was struggling, stressed and anxious because of the way I looked at the world, the way I thought about it. Not only that, but the way I was responding to the world was hampering my ability to make an impact. I was wasting time and energy in worry and stress, so I couldn't be as creative or decisive or skilful as when I was at my best. I wasn't being as effective as I could be.

By shifting my internal experience of the world, the most impactful change happened. Over the following years, I developed a series of ideas that helped me live life less and less from a place of stress, anxiety and exhaustion, and more and more from a place of possibility. I was able to be more skilful, whatever the world threw at me, and make an even bigger contribution. This was vital because, as I started using my strengths, I faced challenges and crises of confidence and self-belief. If you want to make an impact, you will face those challenges, too. The ideas that could shift me to more possibility in those moments of struggle are what I'll share with you in Part One of this book.

I took those ideas and applied them to different parts of my life, especially my career and my romantic relationship. I'll share the specifics of what I learnt as I did that in Part Two.

That, then, is what this book is about: how to create shifts in the outside world and in your internal world so that you can use your strengths to make an impact and feel less stressed and anxious as you do it.

The Complex World

One of the great pleasures of my work as a coach is spending time in the company of some of the leading thinkers in my field. As I was working on a draft of this book, I took part in a training course on the cutting edge of adult psychological development and coaching. In essence, adult psychological development is the process by which we develop our sense of perspective on the world: the different ways of thinking that we go through in our lives. On the simplest level, as we develop, we can see things more clearly and from more angles and perspectives.

I had previously been sceptical of the popular narrative that the world is faster and more complex than ever. I think part of this is because, by the time I entered the world of work, computers were already in existence and smartphones weren't too far behind. For those of an older generation, who remember how different it was before those devices, it is clear just how much things have changed. My work with leaders and entrepreneurs helped me see the truth of the challenges of complexity – time and again, I'd see how the technology and pace of the modern world can lead to incredibly multifaceted, high-pressure situations, and how beneficial it can be to have the voluntary stop of a coaching session to slow down and take stock. Due to the power of modern technology, as more people around the world get connected to the disruptive and innovative powers of the Internet, the change will only accelerate.

In *Unlocking Leadership Mindtraps: How to Thrive in Complexity*, consultant and researcher Jennifer Garvey Berger unpacks the ways that the human brain falls foul of complexity in the modern world. As I read her book, I realised that many of the lessons in it were also the lessons in *this* book.

You see, although I hadn't realised it at the time, I had been working through the challenges of being a human, with a brain evolved for simpler times, in a complex world.

Those challenges are many: we get sidetracked by instinct and caught up in simple ways of looking at the world when more complex ones are needed. Indeed, according to Garvey Berger and other developmental psychologists, it is the increasingly complex nature of the world that is calling us all to develop psychologically, to see things from more angles and with greater perspective.

I had seen this with my clients. So many of the things people wanted, the challenges they faced, seemed almost impossible in the face of complexity. How do you get 'clarity' about what a choice would mean in a world where there are more moving parts than at any point in history? How do you manage your time when the technology we use is designed by the cleverest people on the planet specifically to grab and keep our attention? How do you develop a plan when uncertainty in everything from the job market to the political landscape seems to be on the rise?

In the complexity of the modern world, many of the ways humans have traditionally got through these challenges no longer work: clarity, plans and techniques for managing our time catch us out as often as they help us out[2]. What I learned – and what Garvey Berger and others describe in their work – is that what actually works is to grow your psychological spaciousness. You become more aware of yourself and the world and, therefore, less likely to get sidetracked. You work to become nimbler and more skilful, both in your own internal experience (the world inside you) and outside yourself as you interact with the world. You become more in tune with what you want, deep down, so that when opportunities arise, you can take them (or leave them, whichever is the right choice for you). You become more responsive and responsible for yourself. That was the journey that I had been on.

Indeed, at that crucial moment in my life, it looks to me like the involuntary stop of the break-up and looking at my work life anew accelerated a major developmental change of my psychology: moving from one 'level of development' to another, shifting me into a far more complexity-fit way of seeing the world. It's possible that you are in a moment like that, too, and that reading this book and exploring the ideas here will help you on that path. At least, I hope it does.

Introduction

When I realised that the Adult Development training course covered some of the same ideas I was writing about in this book, I got the answer to the question that Joel and I had asked: is this new way of looking at the world valid? Well, according to some of the leading thinkers in my field, it was not only valid, but it was also vital – for me and for the leaders, entrepreneurs and coaches that I worked with, too. Indeed, it's vital for all of us as we try to survive and then thrive – in ourselves, in our work, in our relationships – in a complex world.

That, too, is what this book is about: how to thrive in every part of our lives in a world of uncertainty and complexity.

Make Things Better... and Don't Make Things Worse

In The Hero's Journey (the pattern of story popularised by Joseph Campbell), just as the hero most needs it, she or he receives supernatural aid. In my journey to writing this book, one moment of supernatural aid arrived as I came across the work of futurist and thinker, Jordan Hall. In a world of increasing complexity, with fears that humanity could make itself extinct through weapons or environmental catastrophe and with political uncertainty seemingly on the increase, what can we do? Hall's answer was straightforward: we each do our best. That, after all, is all we can do. To do that, you must first understand what makes up the unique mix of skills and gifts that only you have and then find the place in the world that needs them, bringing to bear as fully as possible what you have to offer in the place where you can make the biggest impact.

That is the journey I have been on in my own life and it is how and where my work with clients has become more focused. Supporting them to use their strengths and gifts to find – in the phrase coined by psychotherapist, Gay Hendricks – their Zone of Genius.

Then, continues Hall, you must make sure that in each moment you are making the best choice with the highest degree of skill possible. That way, you are doing the best you can to contribute using your Zone of Genius, but more than that: if you are doing your best to contribute *skilfully*, then you know that you are trying to make things better and not worse.

That is also what this book is about: how to make sure you are doing the best you can to make things better and not worse by using your Zone of Genius and using it with skill.

Who Knows How Long We Have to Steady This Ship?

When I started writing this book, I was worried that if it took a long time to come out (which, of course, it has – it's been something like nine years since Joel and I first had that conversation), it would become less and less relevant. Now, it feels like it becomes more relevant by the day.

Institutions that looked like they would last forever a decade ago no longer look so permanent. Global geopolitics seem less stable than at any point in my life. Social media is having strange effects on our mental health, our attention spans and the way we consume news. Concerns about climate catastrophe abound. A global pandemic has changed the way everything works. Each of these problems and more not only seem enormous, but incredibly complex.

To meet these challenges, we need people who can use their strengths to make things better. We need skilful and responsive leaders: in politics, business and charities, yes, but also in homes, schools and communities across the world. It is down to each of us to lead in our lives, to be as responsive and wise as we can and to support others to do the same. We are all on this ship together; who knows how long we have to steady it?

I want this book to illustrate how each of us can live more as our **Higher Self**. Others use different words for this: some call it 'being centred'; Jordan Hall called it 'sovereignty.' It is the state you are in when you are responding from the wisest, noblest and most skilful place in yourself, when you are responding with grace, elegance and strength to whatever life throws at you. It is a place of presence, flow and possibility.

The phrase Higher Self speaks to three crucial elements of the shift that is available to us.

First, our psychological development. The Adult Development theories that resonate so much with the ideas in this book are sometimes called Vertical Development. The metaphor here might be that we can learn horizontally, akin to exploring a landscape a bit at a time, or we can grow vertically. That would be like finding the high ground and seeing, from that different perspective, the lay of the land. As your Higher Self, from the high ground, you can then reach your destination with more skill, speed and poise.

Second, the possibility for inner peace. As I have worked with more and more leaders, I have found myself talking about old-fashioned words like honour and nobility. Indeed, often in my work with leaders and entrepreneurs, I will ask a question: what do you need to do here so that, regardless of the outcome, you will be at peace with yourself? This is a question of honour, which instantly tells us that there are more important things than the outcome, that the journey matters as well as the destination and that living in alignment with our values is of as much or greater importance as getting outward success. So much of what is covered in this book deals with the challenges of *not* being at peace with ourselves, with regret, worry, stress and anxiety. The Higher Self is the version of you who does the things you won't regret. The you who is courageous, wise and honourable when it counts.

Third, the divine. As someone who had a spiritually connected but largely secular upbringing, in a largely secular education system in a largely secular country, I have found it fascinating and difficult in recent years as I gradually became more comfortable with the importance of the mythopoetic language of the divine. Sometimes, to talk about the things we need to talk about, we need the language that faiths and religions hold onto and secular societies mostly abandon. A few years ago, I was delighted to find out that the word 'Namaste' can be translated as 'I see the divine light as it shines through you.' That is what we are aiming for when we use the ideas in this book, both in what we do and the way we do it, our Higher Selves allow the divine light to shine.

There are times in my life when feelings of grace, elegance, strength and possibility make me feel like a completely different person. I behave differently and respond differently: I am clearer and braver and more loving. It is the noblest, wisest part of me. It doesn't really matter if that is because I have a new psychological roadmap from the higher ground, because I am living more in line with my values and leading my life with honour, or because I am connected to the (metaphorical or real) divine. It matters mostly because that is the kind of person I would like others to see me as; the kind of person I am proud to be. That is what it means to be living as my Higher Self.

To live more as our Higher Selves, we have to understand what I call the **Deeper Self**. One of the things that I will explore in this book is how our behaviour is often governed by unconscious or subconscious parts of us – that is, by instincts that we aren't even

Introduction

aware of but that lead us to behave in certain ways. A key part of the journey to spending more time as our Higher Selves is to become increasingly aware of when those deeper instincts are at play. In our Deeper Selves are evolutionary instincts from our ancestors, the safety mechanisms and patterns we learned as children and adolescents, and the rules of communities we are a part of that help us fit in. At times in our history or childhood, these things kept us safe, but some no longer serve us in the complex world we live in as adults today.

As we grow to know our Deeper Selves, we become more aware of these patterns. With greater awareness, we are no longer ruled by them; we can notice them, step outside them and act from a place of perspective. In a complex world, our instincts can swiftly sweep us along, triggering us into behaviours and reactions before we know what is happening. Oftentimes, this is where we respond from the baser parts of ourselves, where we do the things that we end up regretting, where we act without skill and make things worse in our work, our relationships or our world.

Each time my clients or I look inside with curiosity, we learn something new. With greater knowledge of ourselves, we become bigger, more grounded and more in control of our lives and our responses. Whether we learn something good or bad about ourselves, understanding those things – understanding our Deeper Selves – makes us more rooted in who we are and gives us greater or swifter access to our Higher Selves.

I hope what you read here helps you get out of your own way, creating shifts in the outside world and in your internal world so that you can use your strengths to make an impact.

I hope that as you use the ideas here, you find your ways out of the traps of complexity, so that you can thrive in all parts of your life, and particularly the parts that matter most to you.

I hope you can use all of this to put your strengths – your Zone of Genius – to good use to steady the ship we are all on with skill, so you can be as sure as possible you are making things better and not worse.

I hope that, as you read this book, you gain access to new ways of seeing the world, which are as transformational for you as my new ways of seeing have been for me: reducing stress, transforming relationships and allowing you to thrive in an ever-more-complex world.

And I think you'll do this by understanding more about your Deeper Self and living more as your Higher Self.

A Starting Point

This book is a starting point. It may be, I hope, a voluntary stop for some of you. An opportunity for you to take these ideas and create change in your life. I hope, too, that you will make that a change for the better by becoming your noble, skilful Higher Self. I hope you make those changes for yourself, for your loved ones and for the world. I hope you will step up, because the world needs you, too: we need more strong, honourable people acting with elegance and grace across all parts of our societies.

We need you at your best. We need you at your nimblest. We need you at your wisest.

My journey to live increasingly as my Higher Self will, I suspect, never be finished. But what pleases me – and this is true for all the principles in this book – is to be moving onwards in the right direction. I am my Higher Self more this year than I was last year, and far more than I was before that involuntary stop. I am doing better today than I did yesterday and the day before and the day before that, and that is what matters.

Introduction

No one knows which one of us will change or save the world. The chances are that – in a world as large and complex as ours – it will be no single person. It will be all of us together, taking brave and heroic decisions every day in organisations, in schools, in workplaces and in homes across the world, being better today than we were yesterday.

To change the world together, to steady the ship we are all on, we need you to be the best and most skilful you can be. And we need you now.

HOW TO USE THIS BOOK

I work as a coach and – as I sometimes say when explaining what that means – coaching isn't really coaching unless there is some action at the end of it. That's true for this book, too. I don't mind how you take action, but I mind that you do take action.

Those actions can be large or small, whether in the outside world or focused on changing the way you think. You get to choose. But make sure they happen.

Each part of the book contains numerous ideas and insights that I believe you could apply in your life, just as I have applied them in mine, to reduce stress, change your relationships for the better and deal more skilfully with the complexity that the world throws at you.

You will find a summary at the end of each chapter that you can use as a quick reference guide. Each summary contains the key ideas and some of the exercises and practices that are described in each chapter, often in the form of questions or thought experiments. You'll also find lists of further reading, selected links to the work of the key people referenced and other ways to learn more.

Feel free to skip these to get to the next idea, but when you are ready to take action (or when you realise a few weeks after reading the book that you haven't yet made any changes), come back to the chapter summaries.

To help you make this book count, I want to offer two free gifts:

How to Use This Book

- A FREE Action Sheet designed to help you turn the ideas from this book into actions and habits that support you to live more as your Higher Self.

- A FREE eBook containing all the chapter summaries from this book in one place: the key ideas, actions, practices and references from the book condensed into just nine pages.

To get these free gifts visit www.robbieswale.com/power-to-choose-gifts or scan the QR code below.

PART ONE

CHAPTER ONE

YOU CAN CHOOSE

When I was a child, I spent many hours engrossed in 'Choose Your Own Adventure®' books[1]. In this series, you read a part of the story and then, at the bottom of each section, you have a choice about what happens next.

> *You come to the end of the corridor. To the left there is a door; to the right there is a flight of stairs, going up.*
>
> *If you want to go through the door, turn to page 43.*
>
> *If you want to go up the stairs, turn to page 56.*

In a normal novel, we get to read the story told through the characters' eyes. Here, it's a different type of involvement: an active involvement where you affect the outcome.

After the involuntary stop of the break-up that I mentioned in the introduction, and as I learned more about the way I and others worked, I began to notice that there were moments like this in my life – and more of them than I had thought. Most importantly, I gradually realised I didn't have to wait until the end of a chapter to make choices. Even when things seemed difficult and hopeless in a particular moment, I still had at least some power to choose.

That's the key idea of this chapter. Just like in the Choose Your Own Adventure books, **you can choose.** And you can do it far more often than you think.

Life doesn't always feel like this. For reasons ranging from the views our parents hold about themselves or the world to the environments we grow up in, the stories told about 'people like us' and the series of events that life sometimes throws at us, we can find ourselves believing something different. Perhaps we know we can affect some things, but other areas of our lives feel completely fixed: a system set up against us, something 'people like me' simply can't do or the weight of the world leaving us feeling trapped or stuck. Perhaps on our good days, we remember that we can change things in our lives, but on others, we slip into a different space, where things feel completely outside our sphere of influence. We all find ourselves in this state at some points in our lives, a seeming victim of the winds of fate. Whether this occurs gradually or suddenly, regularly or occasionally, it is insidious and powerful, holding us still, keeping us from creating the life we want, stopping us from using our strengths in the world.

Over the course of our upbringing, almost all of us gradually find evidence that we can affect at least some areas of our lives. We see the consequences of our actions; we see we have an impact on what happens to us. If we are lucky, or if we do the right work, we can shift out of the sense of 'life happening to us' and move to a story where *we can choose*. As we shift out of these 'stuck' states and into stories where we are in control, our Higher Selves become more available to us. Life has a way of knocking us out of our Higher Selves, though; there will always be times when things feel out of control again. Finding our ways back in those moments is important work, which we can do alone or with a friend or coach. We can find ways to move from seeing important parts of our world as simply happening to us to seeing that we can be a creator and not a victim of our stories, our circumstances and our world.

Helping people see and then hold onto this sense of agency has the power to affect so many of the challenges we, as individuals and societies, face in the modern world. So much of the disquiet, discontent and disappointment we experience in life comes from a sense that we can't affect the story; a lack of hope when we feel as though our lives are outside our influence. This leaves us unable to express the things we want to express, unable to change things, feeling stuck, exactly here, forever. When we are feeling this way, we often find ourselves responding to the world from our baser instincts, causing harm to those around us, making things worse and not better.

In the aftermath of the break-up I mentioned in the introduction, I was in this state. I was stuck in a place of 'life happening to me' and couldn't see the way forward. Whole parts of my life had been taken out of my control by one of the people I trusted and cared about most in the world. I felt lost, adrift and alone.

I made some changes. A lot, in fact. I moved house, then jobs, then towns. I felt a little better. Sometimes. But mostly, I still felt like life was happening to me. It felt stuck, flat, painful and out of my control.

What began to make a real difference to my experience of life was not the change in my circumstances. Instead, it was finding new perspectives on what had happened. And in those perspectives and the insights I uncovered was a deeper sense that 'I can change this.' Maybe I can do things now that I hadn't been able to do before; maybe next time I can create a better relationship; maybe this experience and what follows can help me become a better man, the kind of man I had always hoped to be.

This was the shift from victim to creator. And as I learned more and found more new perspectives – many of which I'll share throughout this book – I noticed something important: our experience of life is affected not just by what we do, but by what we think, what we assume, the perspectives we take and the stories we tell about ourselves and the world. Taking action out in the world did make a difference, creating changes that took me closer to what I really wanted. But what made a bigger, quicker difference – sometimes almost instantaneously – was changing the way I looked at things, thought about things and responded to things.

I had spent most of my life knowing, at least intellectually, that I could take action and, from that, create change in the outside world, even though it wasn't always easy. Yet despite knowing that, I still found myself regularly scared, anxious and stressed. Sometimes I knew what I wanted to do but was too terrified to do it[2]. At other times, I knew I could change my job, but changing it didn't always make me happy. Or I knew I could create change in my organisation, in my relationship and in the outside world, whether it was in my community or even potentially on a bigger scale. But that didn't feel meaningful or fulfilling. The act of doing more or different things in the outside world can make a world of difference to us, but it isn't everything. Why, for example, do we sometimes see people achieve their 'dreams' yet still end up unhappy? Why do people end up hugely successful in one part of their life, but unsuccessful in the parts they claim matter to them more? Why are some people able to face challenges and emerge stronger, while others face the same things and slip and stumble in a downward spiral?

The idea that *you can choose* can help you affect change in the outside world. If we want our lives to feel meaningful, it is important to set intentions and then make progress towards them. It is important to see your progress and develop confidence that, at least here in this small area, my life is created by me. Taking steps to change things, no matter how small, was what took me out of the hell of making do and muddling through and back into action in the world. It empowered me to believe that in my next relationship, things could be different and to believe that I could make other changes that would take me towards what I really wanted, deep down. Remember, though, that you don't always have to wait for the obvious moment of choice or, if you will, for the end of the Choose Your Own Adventure chapter. Sometimes, *you can choose* something different inside your mind, in the way you think or the way you see the world, and this can create the change you want. Right here, right now. The opportunities to do this are all around us.

One of my clients once spoke to me about her experience of this[3]. Looking to create more autonomy in her life so she could lead her teams and projects more effectively, she no longer wanted to feel trapped and out of control as a result of the pointless meetings she "had to go to." In some cases, she was able to create change in the outside world: to literally stop going to the meetings, sometimes right away and sometimes by making small decisions over a number of months to relinquish roles or to decide only to attend regular meetings some of the time. But what she was able to do *straight away* was to feel differently in the meetings she attended. Sometimes she did this simply by reminding herself of the autonomy and control she had – 'I'm choosing to come here' – and she would feel different. Sometimes it would be more specific: boring as the meeting was, it was progressing her towards an overarching goal or a future role. In choosing to see the meetings differently, she was *instantly* able to feel the agency she had in the situation. That didn't always make the meetings exciting, but it changed her experience of them, making them less unpleasant, enabling her to be more present in each of those meetings and act, in each of them and outside them, less from frustration and more from her Higher Self.

We need both parts of *you can choose* if we are truly to inhabit our skilful, wise Higher Selves and contribute to the world. We need the outside world confidence of 'life can be created by me' and we also need the skill to choose our perspectives in each moment. The first part of this is one of the areas of my work as a coach that I love the most: seeing people develop that confidence or seeing them take it to a new level and create not just small changes, but extraordinary ones. And the second part is the crux of this book: showing you how valuable it is to be able to choose your perspectives in each moment and sharing ideas that enable you to do that.

It's All Invented

As I leaned into this idea that *I can choose*, I saw more of these opportunities to change things in the moment, even without the outside world changing. Key to this was *The Art of Possibility*, a book by Rosamund Stone Zander and Benjamin Zander. The book, based on Ros Zander's work as a family therapist and Ben Zander's experience as a conductor and music teacher, is a beautifully written and deeply touching set of practices designed to help us live more in possibility. Across these practices, it teaches the principle of this chapter: that *you can choose* to live in a place of possibility, not of scarcity. *The Art of Possibility* was where I began to see what a beautiful word 'possibility' is for describing a feeling I recognised from my best moments, a fundamental part of living as my Higher Self.

The Zanders aren't the only thinkers to have written about a version of the idea that *we can choose* – we'll get to others in this chapter and beyond – but the first practice in *The Art of Possibility* is a beautiful one for demonstrating what might be possible for us if *we can choose* in our internal world. That first practice is: 'It's All Invented.' At its core, this practice is to ask ourselves: what if everything we see in the world is invented? If it is, shouldn't we invent some things that are helpful to us?

This may sound far-fetched, but as neuroscience becomes more advanced, we are able to see just how much our brain creates for us, showing us not what is 'actually' happening in the world, but an approximation of it. An example of this is our peripheral vision, which experiments show is a product of approximation on the part of our mind – filling in gaps and making assumptions – rather than showing us what is actually there. It shouldn't come as a surprise that we don't see everything. Broadly we are aware, when we think about it, that there are other creatures with superior senses to us. We know that dogs can smell things that humans can't, that bats can hear things that humans can't. We don't seem to remember this with what we see, however, so it is important to note that there are also creatures that can see 'more' than we can and not just in terms of distance or clarity. Bees, apparently, can make out ultraviolet patterns on flowers; owls (and many other nocturnal creatures) can see far better than we can in the dark. So, if there are things that other creatures can see but we can't, and our brain is only giving us an approximation of what is out there anyway, it seems clear that what we see isn't 'reality.' It is, to a greater or lesser extent, invented.

This idea of 'It's All Invented' becomes even more important when our assumptions start to play tricks on us. *The Art of Possibility* memorably reminds its readers of a famous puzzle (Figure 1): participants are shown a square with nine dots (three rows of three) and asked to 'join all nine dots using four straight lines or fewer, without lifting the pen from the paper and without tracing the same line more than once.' (Try it, if you like, before reading further.)

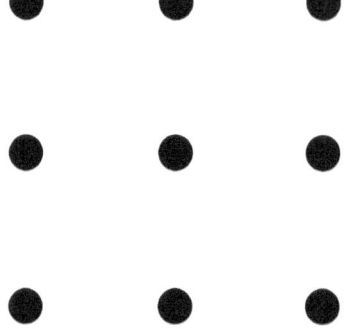

Figure 1: This is the 'nine dots' puzzle: join all nine dots using four straight lines or fewer, without lifting the pen and without tracing the same line more than once.

Almost everyone who tries the puzzle struggles with this because they assume an extra rule without even noticing they do it. They add in, at the end of the task, the words 'without using the space outside the dots.' This added assumption comes because our eyes show us not simply nine dots, but a square, and we assume that the edge of the puzzle is the edge of the square. This happens without us noticing and, with this assumption, the puzzle becomes impossible. Remove the assumption – which, again, we can note was invented by us without our conscious minds thinking about it – and the puzzle suddenly becomes possible[4].

Optical illusions provide a vivid demonstration of how a simple change of perspective can show us something new. In one well-known optical illusion (Figure 2)[5], once we have seen both possibilities, *we can choose* that the picture is an older woman or *we can choose* that the picture is a younger woman.

This is happening to you all the time. Your mind is inventing assumptions that might be making the puzzle of your life impossible to solve, keeping you from seeing perspectives that might make things different. It is happening across your life, from what you literally see through your eyes to your interactions with people every day, to

You Can Choose

Figure 2: Is it an old woman or a young woman? Once you have seen both, you can choose which perspective to take.

how you view yourself, to your relationships, to the world of work. What if, instead, you could see the multiple possibilities available and invent, as the Zanders suggest, something that actually helps you? What if *you can choose*?

One of my favourite moments of the 'It's All Invented' practice in *The Art of Possibility* comes from a later chapter in the book. Ben Zander is teaching a class about leadership to students in a prestigious music school in Boston; he realises that, to help the students think freely and creatively, it's important they aren't trapped into competing with others due to their worries about their grades in the class. But it's also important that they attend the class amidst pressure to get good grades, so he can't simply remove the grading system altogether. To make it worth their while, he guarantees them an A for the course as long as they write to him explaining why they deserve an A and then come to every class in the year. This, it turns out, allows them to think more freely and creatively from a place of possibility. But what demonstrates how 'It's All Invented' is when one of the students shares what has shifted for him. In his former school in Taiwan, he explains, he was ranked 68th out of 70 students. "I come to Boston and Mr Zander says I am an A. Very confusing. I walk about, three weeks, very confused. I am number 68, but Mr Zander says I am an A student… I am Number 68, but Mr Zander says I am an A. One day I discover I am much happier A than Number 68. So I decide I am an A."

Before reading that book, I would have thought that one of these gradings was more real: he was the 68th best in the class. The A for 'writing a letter and showing up' isn't real – that's just a music teacher playing around – but the book showed me another possibility: 68/70 based on what? Based, simply, on a convention: a mutually invented story that it is useful to rank students based on their ability, measured by assessment. The school (actually, another school a long time ago) invented it and we have all gone along with it. It affects how this particular student is, how happy he is, the work he does, how he engages and learns, and who knows what else? Ben Zander recognises that, in this situation, the way it is affecting him isn't helpful and so invents another way to grade the class, and the effect on the student is marked. The student then beautifully chooses the assumption that actually helps him: if he writes the letter and attends the class, he is an A student in that class and can think of himself as such. He realises he can decide. *He can choose.*

You can probably imagine what it is like to be 68/70. To know that you are almost at the bottom of the pile. You can probably imagine the pressure of a prestigious school and the sense that you are failing. This can be useful: it can make you resolve to lift yourself up the list[6]. Sometimes, however, the scarcity of competition stops us from seeing what is important, stops us from thinking clearly, from doing our best work and from enjoying life. In this case, 68/70 wasn't even the rank of the student in *that* school, it was his rank from his previous school being carried by the student as a definition of himself as a person; it was an unconscious part of his Deeper Self. At the very least, it sounds like it was stopping him enjoying his education in Boston. At the worst, it may well have been hindering his learning, creativity, decision-making, relationships and general way of thinking. The shift to the A instead may have opened up his potential in all these areas and more. And what possibility there is then! Suddenly, he can look at these two options and decide which is more useful. Which allows him more freedom or creativity? Which spurs him on to perform better? Which makes him happy? The notion of 68/70, for most of us, does not allow us the freedom or responsiveness or happiness we desire, but the possibility of the A and the access to our Higher Selves it unlocks is something different.

Try this for yourself. For many of us, being ranked according to our competence doesn't happen much when we are adults, although those in certain professions (salespeople, for example) may find themselves ranked in line with targets. As children and students, it was much more common. Take yourself back to a time you ranked low down a list that mattered to you, a time when you were disappointed with the result. A time when it hurt. Perhaps it was in a maths test or an art exam, perhaps a time you were picked last or near last in sport, perhaps when you were given the smallest part in a play or didn't even make the cast. Take yourself back to that time, remember being ranked like that, tell the story to yourself: I was 21st out of 22 in football; the best 30 performers were selected and I wasn't, so I am 31st at best; I came 120th out of 140 in my year. Take yourself right back to that moment and see how it feels. See if you can remember how much access you had to the skilful, wise, creative parts of you. Then, see what might happen when you invent an assumption. Make it one that could be true: if you *had* to give yourself an A for your role in that situation, how and why would you do so? See what changes for you as you find that reason.

My story at university was a little like the inverse of Ben Zander's Taiwanese student. At school, I was the best at maths in the year. I learnt this when we had a standardised test aged 14 and I came top, a couple of points ahead of the next student. Being top of the class was my story about mathematics and it served me well. It spurred me on and filled me with confidence and I scored very highly at GCSE and A Level. I then went on to study undergraduate mathematics at University College London, one of the top-ranking universities for maths in the UK. Something was different at university. It was painful to find out that I wasn't so talented after all. In my first year, I struggled with my university work just as much as I struggled with settling into life in one of the biggest cities in the world. I stuck it out and passed the year, limping to mainly Cs and Ds. It was a relief in the end not to fail the year altogether.

Simply passing would not have been acceptable to the person I was in my A-level year, but I found myself reframing the story. In the Zanders' terms, I found the way to give myself an A for passing the year. I was a Grade A student because I put in the effort; I stuck it out despite the shock to the system of the different style of learning required and the struggles I had adapting to life away from home. I was a Grade A student for what I did outside of my test scores.

The key here is that this story was not about making excuses for my failure. It instead allowed me to see clearly what I was gaining from my time as a student. Is my literal grade all that matters at university? If it is, not being an A-grade student is demoralising and painful and the right decision might be to give up, leave and find something else to study. If my literal grade *isn't* all that matters, then I can see the value in how hard I had worked, and the value in the way I had made friends, made connections and begun to live a fulfilling life outside of my studies. This new story was powerful for me: instead of being a literal Grade A student, I can give myself an A for passing despite everything; *I can choose* what is important to me. This meant that by the time I failed two exams in my second year (I don't think I'd *ever* failed an exam before that), it didn't faze me; it was clear to me that that wasn't what mattered. I was a Grade A student if I was making a contribution to university life, if I was making friends that might last for decades, if I was going on adventures, growing as a person and having lots of fun. And I did all these things. Not only that, but they were what led to me being elected as co-president of UCL Students' Union, which, in turn, led to my first job out of university as director and trustee of an organisation that turned over £2 million and employed hundreds of people. And the lower second-class grade of my degree didn't affect that at all.

So, take the time to rewrite your stories of disappointment. Look at a situation through the perspective of your old story and then try to find the ways in which you can give yourself an A: as a footballer who played as well as you could, even though you were picked last; as a performer who was vulnerable and courageous to sing in front of people and be judged, despite not having the training that some others did; as a student who improved their ranking from 120 one year to 100 the next. Again, the aim is not to give yourself an easy ride: the game is to shift your perspective between different assumptions just as you can shift the way you look at an optical illusion. See what changes; see if the puzzle of your life becomes easier to solve.

If 'It's All Invented' anyway, isn't that the obvious thing to do?

The Rational Optimist

Reading *The Rational Optimist* by Matt Ridley was another important step for me in learning that *I can choose*. Whilst *The Art of Possibility* gave me many tools and philosophies to make my shift into a life of more possibility, to shift in any moment towards my Higher Self, Ridley's book gave me something different.

First, it showed me that there is another way of looking at our world. I had learned in all sorts of ways, including by the bias of news media towards negative stories, to look on the modern world as one of depravity and greed, always on the edge of disaster. In *The Rational Optimist*, however, Ridley paints a different picture. He tells story after story with convincing, rational, broad arguments and plenty of evidence, which opened my mind to alternative viewpoints on topics that had felt closed to me. Ridley's clear and rational approach showed me that it's possible to make assumptions that are different from the ones I was making on everything, from trade to economic problems in Africa, politics and climate change, guided and backed up each time by evidence. You don't have to believe all (or, indeed, any) of the stories he tells, but if you can read them even as possibilities, this suddenly opens up the idea: what if some of these are true?[7] I had thought these issues were settled and that there was only one way to look at them. Ridley's storytelling and research opened me up to the possibility that there was more.

This is straight out of the Adult Development theorists' work that I described in the introduction: certainties and black-and-white thinking creating a worldview that doesn't capture the nuance of the real world. Minds that evolved for simpler times defaulting to simple stories when shades of grey are needed to see the world in a more complexity-fit way.

In one particularly memorable section of *The Rational Optimist*, Ridley describes a cosy, Dickensian family scene. Children and parents are huddled round a fire in their living room, one of them reading and a bird singing outside. It is the kind of scene that makes me smile, reminding me of costume dramas on the BBC and of a simpler time without a buzzing phone or a slew of unanswered emails. It sounds idyllic. He then opens up statistically what might have happened to that family: the father unlikely to live into his 50s; clothes ridden with lice; the baby to die of smallpox; toothache for the mother; no light other than the fire because candles are too expensive; the bird singing outside to be trapped by the family and eaten the next day because they are hungry and food is scarce.

Which is true, then? Was it an idyllic, simpler time or was it horrible and painful compared to a modern fireside scene? Perhaps both? Or neither? The question you might want to consider is: as you compare the stories, what happens to how you feel about your life? What happens to how you feel about the world? What possibilities does each open and close?

In another reframing of assumptions in *The Rational Optimist*, I had believed that one of the challenges facing the world was overpopulation, that the world was impossibly crowded and due to get more so. I had believed that we were likely to run out of food and other resources because of this. I learned from Ridley that, although no one knows for sure why, population growth is slowing. Moreover, people have been saying for centuries that we would run out of resources due to population growth and, yet, food hasn't run out on a global scale (although, of course, there are many people who still do not have enough). To demonstrate just how false my assumption was of the planet being impossibly crowded, it is worth pausing on a rather illustrative story: if we gave every person in the world a house of average size, all of those houses would fit into the area of the US state of Texas. This is so counterintuitive that I have checked the maths on it several times and, to my continuing surprise, it seems to add up[8]. If we all lived in Texas, it wouldn't allow for much space to move around in terms of roads or gardens, though. We'd need a couple of Texases for that, and a bit more space for when the population reaches 9-11 billion, where experts say it is likely to peak, but suddenly the planet doesn't seem so small.

And so, what happens when you shift between two different perspectives about the population of the world? You can do this, just like you might switch between the view of the young woman or the old woman in the optical illusion, or from being 68th out of 70 to being an A-grade student. One point of view is that the world is massively crowded, people are bound to starve and there are just too many people around. Another is that there is an enormous amount of space to fit even 11 billion people in and we haven't run out of food, despite centuries of worrying about it, because, essentially, we have become far more efficient at creating food from the resources we have available. In fact, we seem to be successfully feeding more and more people every year.[9]

I give the examples above about the Victorian fireside scene and overpopulation not to try to persuade you of a certain viewpoint, but to show that there are assumptions taking place in each moment, about things as notable as history and the population of the planet. *You can choose* which story to believe and choosing differently can change how you see the world and how you feel about it. Seeing these assumptions allows us to more skilfully make choices that reflect where the greater evidence might be. That, really, is the key part of upgrading our psychological operating system to a more complexity-fit way of seeing the world: taking two stories that are too simple, or an assumption we hadn't been aware we were making, and reconstituting them with greater awareness into something that more closely reflects reality.

Through seeing the different assumptions and recognising that none of them is 'true,' *you can choose* the stories that best support you to have the life you want to have and perhaps to live more as your Higher Self.

Suffering Is Never Caused by What Is Actually Here Now

I am lucky to have learned from many great teachers. One of those whose work almost instantly shifted the way I thought was Jim Dethmer, co-author of *The 15 Commitments of Conscious Leadership*, who I have been lucky to be on several online workshops with over the years. In one workshop, Dethmer took my fellow students and me through a practice he teaches to all the leaders he works with. It is to set up an app (Mind Jogger for Apple users or RemindMe for those with Android) to ask a certain number of times a day: 'Robbie, what is actually here now?'

Dethmer says there are only three categories of things that can *actually* be here now: sensory experience (including emotion), thoughts and a sense of a personal self[10]. Once you have noticed what is actually here now, you ask yourself a follow-up question: 'Can I accept what is here now?' The reason for Dethmer's questions lies in a modern articulation of ancient Buddhist and Stoic wisdom: that psychological suffering is never caused by what is actually here now. Instead, it is caused by *resisting* what is actually here now.

This is a big idea. It gives us the possibility that our psychological suffering is caused by our response to what happens in our lives, not by things that happen outside us. This can feel incredibly jarring to consider, but if 'It's All Invented' (if it even *might* be all invented), then you have a choice. You can assume that your pain is caused by things outside you and your control, including people. In this case, you remain a victim, with your pain or struggle outside of your sphere of influence. Or you can assume that, by responding differently, you can reduce, remove or change your pain and make your experience of life better. The adventure I am inviting you on is the latter: *you can choose* that your pain is caused by your response to what is actually there in those moments.

When Dethmer shared this idea in the training course, I had a moment of 'ah, this one again.' Because I'd heard it before, through popular culture and other learning. I had always found it hard to grasp, but this time, I was able to grasp it and hold it with a deeper understanding. That was because earlier that year, with the ideas in this book in my mind, I had decided to test *you can choose* when I caught a cold.

I am someone who, in my life up to that point, really hated being ill. It affected me mentally and physically. My frustration at not functioning at 100% was enormous and had been for years. I hated that I couldn't make the most of my time because I was ill. I hated that I was missing out on things. I hated that I couldn't even enjoy the things I enjoy. Beer, for example, isn't a sensible thing to drink when you are ill, and when unwell I sometimes couldn't focus enough to lose myself in my latest fantasy novel. So, when I started to develop a cold while writing a draft of this chapter, I decided to try applying *you can choose* to my life in a new way: what would happen if I chose to *enjoy* being ill? And I was genuinely astounded at the result. I felt better. Not totally better – I still had the physical symptoms of a cold – but it suddenly became clear to me just how much of the bad feeling when I was ill was because I was *resisting* the cold. I was resenting it. I was wishing it wasn't there. My mind was full of thoughts of scarcity ('I'm missing out,' 'I'm wasting time') and regret ('I wish I didn't have this,' 'If only I could drink a beer guilt-free'). By this time, I was reasonably practiced at shifting perspectives and was able to do it swiftly: I stopped resisting. It's interesting, in some ways, that that's all there really is to it: there isn't a secret. I simply shifted my viewpoint, just as I can do with the picture of the old woman and the young woman or with the story about the Dickensian family. However, that isn't quite the full story.

Whilst the core principle of this chapter is simple, it is not always easy. What made my shift of perspective about my cold work so well was that I had a constant and regular reminder of what I was choosing. What happened was that every time someone asked me how I was, I told them the story I am telling you here. I would say: "I'm ill, but I've decided to stop hating having a cold and it seems to make it a lot better!" I'm not sure how many people believed me or tried it for themselves, but each time I told the story, I found myself smiling, laughing even, at the ridiculousness of it all. And they were laughing, too, at how I had spent every cold up to that point in my life resisting…and suffering more as a result.

This is what Dethmer's practice using Mind Jogger or RemindMe does: it gives a regular reminder not to resist what is actually here now; it is an invitation to accept what is present in each moment instead.

Another powerful practice to avoid resisting what is present is to ask yourself the question: 'What is the gift in this situation?' This question opens up the possibility of a different perspective from the one that you are initially experiencing. Perhaps the gift of a different cold is to be able to stay in bed and watch Netflix without worrying what you should do round the house. Or perhaps it is to make you slow down, to allow you the chance to not work yourself to the bone and to protect you from a bigger burnout. This is not to say that the physical symptoms disappear: this is simply to give yourself the opportunity to choose a perspective that includes what is real about the symptoms and perhaps some gifts, too.

Of course, life can sometimes hit you hard and it can be incredibly difficult to do this, at least in the moment. A serious illness, for example, could affect you physically and psychologically for a longer period and make it very hard to find gifts in the situation. Even then, though, many people tell stories about how a risk to their health was the catalyst they needed to change things for the better. Whilst they wouldn't wish the illness on anyone else, they can feel gratitude for what they took from it: finding the gift in their involuntary stops, as I found the gift in mine.

Above all, though, I tell these stories about physical illness because they illustrate that the options for choosing our own internal adventure are almost endless. They can have an almost instant effect on anything from our ability to solve a problem (like the 'nine dots' puzzle) to the way we see the world (like changing our story about overpopulation) to something as tangible as how ill we feel. It's up to us to play and to practise.

Thought Taking Form in the Moment

Sunday Times bestselling author, Jamie Smart, explains in his work how he believes that everything about our experience of life is caused by thought taking form in the moment. He believes that even your emotions start from thought and, with a full understanding of this, you can change the way you experience life beyond recognition. He and the many people whose lives have been changed by his work and work along similar lines by others, such as Michael Neill and Sydney Banks, think the realisation of this and the ways it can help people out of their psychological problems will be a psychological revolution. Smart, in particular, believes that in this idea lies the principles for ending psychological problems and that, one day, people will look back at us like we do at people who believed the world was flat or who treated disease by bleeding the infirm. This, again, may seem like a big idea, but it is clear that therapists, psychologists and coaches across the world work with the beliefs, thoughts and assumptions we have, all of which take place inside us. I do this work with clients: we work on the way they see the world, changing it through conversation and through taking action to create change. Remember that, as the old saying goes, we see the world not as it is but as we are.[11]

I see the change in my clients and the results that follow while their stories about themselves and others change, just as I see the changes in myself. This is truly amazing if you think about it. In essence, the central process in coaching and psychotherapy is that our stories about ourselves change or become more conscious and the feedback that a coach or therapist gets can be extraordinary. One of my friends, for example, talks about how psychotherapy *saved his life*.[12]

Our assumptions and beliefs have a huge hold over us and they are things that we can change.

The Honour Question

The author and consultant, Fred Kofman, whose work we will return to in the next chapter, gives us a powerful frame to take the ideas in this chapter out into the world. It was when watching a session of Kofman's that I first heard the question I shared in the introduction: what do you need to do here so that, regardless of the outcome, you will be at peace with yourself?

It's important to know that just because *you can choose* far more than you thought, you don't necessarily get everything you want. Even when we take responsibility, shift away from a 'victim' mindset and into a 'creator' mindset, the complexity of the world may take outcomes out of our control. We can do our best and still not get the job, not have the person agree to go out with us, not make the sale, not pass the test. In the face of this, *we can choose* to focus on what really matters to us: on what Kofman calls 'success beyond success.'

The power of Kofman's question is that whilst we don't have control over the outcomes in our lives, we always have control over whether we choose to act from the higher parts of ourselves.

We can ask ourselves that question and it always boils down to: did I do what it was wise to do and give what it was wise to give, in an honourable way, in pursuit of my goal? Or did I compromise myself in pursuit of that goal?

Or, in other words: did I live in alignment with the values that matter most to me? Did I live as my Higher Self?

I think of this question as The Honour Question. Honour is about doing the right thing, the thing aligns with our Higher Selves, even when it's hard, and, crucially, not compromising that in pursuit of some external result. No external result will be worth that compromise.

The Honour Question also forces us into a more realistic view on what is within our control: not what we wish was in our control, but what is actually within our sphere of influence. That, as with Dethmer's prompt, brings us closer to what is actually here now.

This means that by using The Honour Question, *you can choose* to guide your actions towards the actions of the Higher Self in the outside world. *You can choose* a way of thinking that will relieve pressure, suffering and stress by removing the false belief that everything is within your control and focusing you instead on what is *actually* within your realm of influence.

You can do that by asking: what do I need to do here so that, regardless of the outcome, I will be at peace with myself?

No matter how rough the seas are in the outside world as you work to make an impact, it is always within your control to choose to do everything you can to act as your skilful, noble, honourable Higher Self.

As you do that, you may find you are more successful and suffer less in the process.

We Can Choose

Through the stories I have told here and in the rest of this book, through my work with clients and through extensive reading and learning about people, I have learned that *I can choose*. Through all this, I have grown my understanding of what it is to be me and what it is to be human.

This chapter contains the underlying principle that will enable you to change your world. We do not have to be victims of our lives in the outside world. When we see possibility, when we have the right support, *we can choose* to change our situation, change our job, change our relationship. We can set an intention and work towards it. We can take charge and be the creator of our lives. Even more importantly, just as we do not have to be victims of circumstance in the outside world, we do not have to be victims of our assumptions and stories inside our minds, inside ourselves. *We can choose* how to respond, inside and out.

If we live a little more as our Higher Selves each day or week or month, we can create the change we want to see in the outside world, even if only a little at a time. We can create the change we want to see in the inside world, too. In fact, our power is even greater there.

Even if you don't quite believe me, ask yourself this: wouldn't you prefer it if I was right? Wouldn't you prefer to choose to feel a feeling of possibility more often? Isn't that a story worth trying on or an assumption worth inventing?

You will see over the coming chapters that the rest of this book is based on this principle. At each stage of my journey, as I have developed ways to understand things with greater perspective, I have increasingly been able to choose which perspective serves me best in each moment and which is fitter for the complexity of the world. Each chapter to follow will give further guidance on ideas and attitudes I believe are worth choosing if you want to live more as your Higher Self and create more of the life you want.

Above all, I want you to take away from this chapter that *we can choose* what we think and, more than that, *we can choose* how we think.

How Do I Do This?

It could certainly be argued that the ideas in this chapter are all you need: away you go and get on with it, happy forever more! My experience has been different, though. In fact, the idea that 'I just need to think differently' has at times sent me wild with frustration.

An insight is only as good as the way it is used and the insight that *we can choose* must be used repeatedly throughout our lives in order to have the kind of effect that will be transformative. We have to choose to think differently so many times that it becomes our *instinct* to think in ways that are more useful to us, to think in ways that allow us to live more and more as our Higher Selves. Yes, for some people and in some cases, the insight that *we can choose* to think in a different way can have an almost instant transformative effect, reducing stress, changing a relationship or increasing joy. That has sometimes been true for me and it will be for you if you start to experiment. The power of *you can choose*, however, is mostly as something to practise every day. It has taken extensive experimentation across my life to find the methods that make the biggest difference. It has then taken practising over and over again to embed those into the way I am, to gradually increase my complexity-fitness, one choice at a time. I expect it will be the practice of a lifetime.

As you embed this into your life, you will regularly be faced by choices: choices of whether to continue in the patterns of thinking or behaviour that have been yours up to this point in your life, or to choose something different. Each time you are ill, someone upsets you or you hear a new perspective on how the world works, you have the power to choose.

If you want things to be as they have always been, think as you have always thought.

If you want things to be different, choose a new adventure.

CHAPTER ONE SUMMARY

Key idea: *You can choose* and you can do it far more than you think. *You can choose* to change things in the outside world, but you can also choose to change the assumptions you make and the perspectives you take. We see the world as we are, not as it 'actually' is, and sometimes choosing a different adventure inside your mind, rewriting invented rules or assumptions, can, in itself, create the change you want. The opportunities to do this are all around us.

Exercises, practices and questions for reflection:

- **Do work to develop the embodied confidence that life is created by you.** Find some small area of your life, no matter how small: anything from how tidy your room is to your diet or your career. Find one that could be different and that you would like to be different. Identify the smallest possible ways in which you could improve it this week. Be realistic and then do those things. At the end of the week, reflect on your progress, notice what worked and what didn't. Then identify the smallest possible ways in which you could improve it next week. Confidence is a result of the action we take: a practice like this will grow the confidence in you that you can change things.

- **What if everything we see in the world is invented?** If it is, what if you are able to choose a different adventure and invent, as Ros and Ben Zander suggest, something that actually helps you?

- **Examine the assumptions you are making**, especially when you find yourself feeling stuck or when things seem black and white.

What am I assuming here? What else could I choose to believe? What else could I choose to think? Is there another assumption that would be more useful? Can I reconstitute these assumptions into something bigger and less black and white? In particular, is there a story or assumption that would allow me more of whatever I feel I am lacking or give me more access to my Higher Self?

- **Give yourself an A.** Next time you find yourself scored low on a list, see how it feels. See how much access you have to your Higher Self. Then, see what happens when you invent an assumption. Make it one that could be true: if you had to give yourself an A for the part you played when you scored badly, how and why would you give yourself the A? See what changes for you as you find that reason. Ask someone for help if this is difficult.

- **What is actually here now?** Set up Mind Jogger or RemindMe to ask you this question at random points throughout the day. Then, once you have an answer, ask yourself: **can I accept what is actually here now?** See what happens if, instead of resisting, you accept what is actually here in this moment.

- **What is the gift of this situation?** Perhaps, by choosing to see the gift in a challenging situation, your perspective will shift and your experience will change. Find an answer that feels true for you, as other people's suggestions on this can sometimes feel patronising. To help find the gift, it can be useful to consider: what is it about this situation that I'm grateful for? What am I learning from this situation? Sit with the questions and see if you can find the gift, no matter how small it seems. When you see it, what is different?

- **Ask yourself The Honour Question.** What do I need to do here so that, regardless of the outcome, I will be at peace with myself? Notice how it changes how you feel about a situation, especially one that might seem overwhelming or out of your control.

- **Remember: you can choose.** In each moment, you have far more choice about your experience of life than you think you do.

Further Reading and Learning

- *The 12-Minute Method Series* by Robbie Swale
- *The Art of Possibility* by Rosamund Stone Zander and Benjamin Zander
- *The Rational Optimist* by Matt Ridley
- *The 15 Commitments of Conscious Leadership* by Jim Dethmer, Diana Chapman and Kaley Klemp
- *The Meaning Revolution* by Fred Kofman

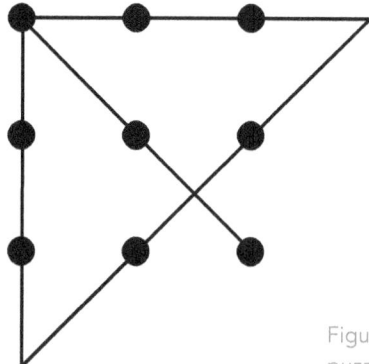

Figure 3: A solution to the 'nine dots' puzzle from earlier in the chapter.

CHAPTER TWO

WHAT IF EVERYONE IS DOING THEIR BEST?

If this book is about living more and more as our Higher Selves – the person we are on our best days, when we are skilful, responsive and graceful as we interact with the world – then one of the most important areas of our lives to explore is how we interact with each other. If this book is about using our strengths, about thriving in complexity and about separating ourselves from our patterns and evolutionary instincts, then one of the most important places to explore is how we relate to other people. And if there is one place where most of us want to make things better not worse, it is in our relationships with the people who matter to us.

We humans are ultra-social animals. For millennia, our ability to cooperate and relate to one another has kept us alive. From tribes hunting on the plains to the many modern tribes, like the organisation we work in or the sports team we support, we are bound into powerful groups that have enormous impact on our lives. We have many interactions with other people in an average week and any of these, whether with someone we live with or someone we meet once and may never see again, has the potential to affect our day, our work and our world. If you're anything like me, you will have regularly seen evidence of this across your life. You will have seen it in the times you have fumed for hours about an inconsiderate stranger and in the times when you have been cheered up by a joke from a checkout worker in a shop you only visit once a year. You will have found your days affected by the postman you see every week and the sibling you have known since you were born. The relationships with those around us can influence us in so many ways, including challenging or inviting our Higher Selves. Indeed, one way to think about your Higher Self is in relation to others: have you been a person you are proud to be, the kind of person you want others to see you as? Have you been the person you want to see reflected in the eyes of those around you?

It Is Our Response to Others That Affects Us

In Chapter One, I shared the idea that *we can choose*, inside and out, as a way to reduce stress and increase access to our more skilful Higher Self. As I took this idea out into the world, it swiftly became apparent that the way I related to others was often causing me anxiety and stress and making me less effective. It was making me less skilful at influencing and communicating and more often wrapped up in my thoughts and worries, unable to act due to anxiety or frustration. In Chapter One, I suggested that it is resisting what is here in any moment that causes us suffering. That is as true in our relationships with others as anywhere else.

Are there places where your interactions with others are affecting your mood, your life and what is happening for you? If this changed, would your life be easier, happier and less stressful? Would better relationships with those around you help you get more done in the world? Would your behaviour be more often in alignment with the kind of person that you want to be? Would you spend more of your time as the adult, clear, creative version of you? Would you, in other words, act more as your Higher Self?

For most people, the answers here are resounding yeses. These things have more impact on us than almost anything else. So, I'm delighted to share with you the most useful tool I have found for dissolving the feeling of scarcity and adversity that can come in our reactions to others. It is the most impactful idea I know for shifting into a place of calm, strength and possibility in relationships with other people. It is a question: *what if everyone is doing their best?*

This question and others like it have fundamentally changed my relationships and enabled me to live far more as my Higher Self. It has changed things for clients in the moment and as a practice over many months.

What if everyone is doing their best? – the key idea of this chapter – invites compassion, care and patience with those around us. It also empowers us to skilfully stand up for what is right, be direct and speak the truth even when it is uncomfortable. It allows our Higher Selves to be far more present, even in the complexity of the 21st century. It allows us to integrate the direct side of us with the caring side, the compassion with the speaking of uncomfortable truth.

Holding these things in balance isn't easy and I have struggled with it all my life. How is it possible to integrate these things and do both at once? How can I stand up for myself without slipping straight into my pettier or more harmful patterns and reactions? It turns out that all of these things are easier when choosing a particular assumption: when I assume that the person I am speaking to is doing their best.

When I Couldn't Sleep

A stark example of the power of this assumption for me comes from perhaps the first time that I truly realised the potential of putting ideas like the ones in this book into practice. I was lying awake, unable to sleep. Time was ticking on. Midnight gone, 1am approaching…then passing. My morning alarm and a day of work were getting closer and closer. My mind wouldn't stop whirring and, more than that, my chest was full of tension. A sense of breathless tightness, of being trapped, so familiar to me at the time.

It is a feeling we might call a 'contraction' and it is a clear signal of being out of my Higher Self in a place of scarcity, of 'life happening to me.' Sometimes when that kind of feeling comes upon us we can't easily draw the line of cause and effect. Then we have to really engage our curiosity about ourselves, as I will discuss more in Chapter Three. This time, though, I knew the origin: it was a conversation on Twitter. Not with just anyone, but with two people I know and respect in real life. Two people who I'd spent many hours with over the years.

I had retweeted an article about the decline in absolute poverty in the world, which felt like good news (because it's gone down a lot). I was in a phase of using the ideas in this book to question the stories I had, especially those that may have originated in the bad news bias of the media. In light of that, it felt important to share something good that was happening. In return, I received a barrage of tweets from one of my friends, expressing how it made him mad because of the authors of the article: he felt they were only sharing it because of a pro-free market economic agenda and accused me of wilfully only sharing articles that pursued that same agenda. I've just been back to the tweets as I write this sentence and, even years later, I can feel some of that same contracted feeling in my chest.

I suggested I was sharing it because it was good news, but was accused by the second friend, arriving 10 or 11 tweets into the exchange, of ignoring the point. Even now, I can't help but read my messages as balanced and theirs as aggressive and angry and mean. Part of that, of course, is that I remember the impact this exchange had for me. I felt tiny, my views mocked, accused of things that weren't true and unable to express what I wanted. The medium of Twitter (or X) doesn't help at times like this: the limit of 140 characters (as it was then) was suitable for headlines, but never for sophisticated or nuanced conversations.

I can see now that many stories were at play here: my friends' assumptions about me, mine about them and, indeed, mine about me. After the exchange, I went to bed, but I definitely didn't sleep.

Hours later, in the middle of the night, still awake, I switched my bedside light on again and saw by the side of my bed the book *The Art of Possibility*, which I discussed in Chapter One. I had enjoyed reading it so much and thought to myself: 'This is a book of practices. There must be something in it to help me right now.'

I opened the book and scanned the headings, my eyes coming to rest on the chapter 'Giving an A.' As the authors explain, this isn't just a practice that can be used in a music college[1] and it isn't always about giving *yourself* an A. When you have a difficult relationship, they suggest, what if you assume that this person deserves an A for their performance in that relationship? If you assume this, how does their behaviour look then? This, at its core, is a very similar question to: what if this person is doing their best?

In one of the most touching moments in *The Art of Possibility*, Ros Zander tells the story of how using this practice to think differently about her deceased father allowed her to understand his behaviour in a way she had never been able to before. If he was a Grade A father, why, then, would he have done what he had done? Using this practice, she even began to remember and notice new things, which added up with this new story.

'Well,' I thought, looking at the book, 'if these people are Grade A friends, why would they be sending me these tweets?' And the answer came back: a great friend would want their friends to understand the world and, for me, a great friend would want the world to be a better place, to put in place the systems and policies that would improve it. At least, that's a requirement I would have for someone who was going to be my Grade A friend. A Grade A friend would call their friends out if their friend was being misled or was behaving badly. A Grade A friend would want to help me gain a deeper understanding of the world.

As I imagined these Grade A motivations for my friends, the feeling of contraction dissipated. Not completely, but these possible qualities in my friends were qualities I could get behind. I could see how they might be doing their best. Before the practice, I had assumed – certainly, it was an assumption, no matter how well I may think I know these people – fury from them and judgment of me. I was telling myself a story that they thought I was stupid, naïve and foolish. I had assumed they were laughing at me together. And those things hurt.

Choosing to see them as Grade A friends made the whole thing look different. With the assumption that they were doing their best for me and themselves and the world, I could choose to look at these friends as people who wanted to challenge me and share their point of view. I could see them as people who were, as they said, joking with me or playing with me. I could see them as people who want the world to be a better place for everyone rather than as people hell-bent on making me feel awful and bullying me into taking their viewpoint.

With that second set of assumptions, the sense of being trapped dissipated, the contraction opened and, remarkably, I drifted off to sleep.

You can see how this different assumption made a positive difference for me, but you might also be wondering: what is the truth here? Well, sitting down years later, my best guess is that the 'Grade A' assumption wasn't quite right, but that the truth lay somewhere *much closer* to that than to my initial assumption. These people, after all, are good people with whom I have spent many hours. In the cold light of day, they like me. They do care about the world, about keeping me honest, about all those things in the 'Grade A friend' definition. *And they weren't particularly kind or skilful in how they acted.*

By looking for a second story that could be behind their behaviour – giving them an A – I was able to make what I believe was a clearer and more truthful assessment of what was happening: a third story, containing both my initial assumptions and my Grade A description. That third story was a more accurate picture of reality: more grey than black or white; more fit for the complexity I was dealing with in that situation.

Without that shift, this situation might have become resentment carried with me from that interaction into the next time I saw these people, as it had for me on many other occasions. Instead, it could dissipate and, in the end, I know that, as my Higher Self, the person I am when I am my best, I am able to have difficult conversations about things like politics. If one of the stories I tell myself makes me feel judged and makes me judge others, *and* it hampers my ability to make a clear and truthful assessment of what is happening, *and* it stops me from having conversations I want to have, then that is not a story taking me towards my Higher Self. Better, by far, to choose something different.

My Life Is Better When I Assume that People Are Doing Their Best

'Giving an A' could almost have been a key principle of this book and is a helpful way to unpack this chapter's central idea. So, too, is a maxim I first heard from writer and podcaster, Tim Ferriss: 'Never put down to malice what you can put down to incompetence or busyness.²' This, too, is a good way to check your assumptions and to give yourself a better chance of living in a space of possibility instead of pent-up fury, resentment and stress.

Ferriss's maxim often brings to my mind my experience with a colleague years ago. She would *never* reply in a timely fashion to my emails. It used to infuriate me: she clearly didn't give the slightest damn about how hard my life was made by having to constantly chase her for things while she did whatever else it was that she did. I had been feeling this tension and frustration over months of working with her, when a co-worker happened to observe that the colleague in question had *thousands* of unread emails in her inbox. Whether this was down to busyness or incompetence in managing her emails, it doesn't matter. What was clear was that her failure to reply was far more likely to be down to incompetence or busyness than that she didn't care about my work specifically.

It seems interesting that, just like with my friends on Twitter, my instant reaction was to assume something deliberately malicious on the part of others. Assuming either incompetence or busyness or both was certainly preferable to the alternative story I had created: that she was making my life harder because she thought my work was so worthless or pointless that it wasn't even worth replying to me. It's much easier, after all, to be around, work with or even like someone who is incompetent than it is someone who you believe actively dislikes or disrespects you. Before long, I began to notice other ways in which this colleague was disorganised and the incompetence angle seemed increasingly likely[3]. That enabled me to be more patient, develop better ways of working with her and even give her extra support.

Both the Zanders' practice and Ferriss's framing are powerful tools for practising this idea in your everyday life, but they weren't

What If Everyone Is Doing Their Best?

what clearly and crisply embedded the idea for me. That happened when I went to see sociologist Brené Brown speak at the British Museum in London in November 2015. Brown is one of the most present and engaging speakers I've ever seen and, over the course of an hour or so, she made an audience of several hundred laugh, cry and change their perceptions and perspectives. She was there promoting her book, *Rising Strong*, an examination of what people who come back from adversity have in common.

'What's the question you have been asked the most about this book?' asked the interviewer at the event.

Brown replied with something like: "Well, it's about 'we're all doing the best we can.' People say: 'Do you really mean everyone? Even this jerk I work with?'"

You may have similar thoughts as you read this chapter.

As Brown said this, we all laughed. The interviewer delved further and Brown told the story, which she also tells in *Rising Strong*, about how people who get back up when they have faced adversity often have something in common regarding their attitude to other people. In short, they live through the assumption that everyone is doing the best they can. Everyone she found who held this belief was someone who she had identified as 'wholehearted,' as people who are willing to be vulnerable and who believe in their self-worth. People who didn't believe this, according to Brown's research, were often also people who struggled with perfectionism. In testing this while, at this point, still thinking it was complete nonsense herself, Brown spoke to her husband, Steve, a paediatrician. He, it turned out, was among the strange group of people who held that view.[4]

Brené asked him her research question about it: 'Do you think that, in general, people are doing the best they can?'

Steve thought about it for 10 minutes, before replying: 'I don't know. I really don't. All I know is that my life is better when I assume that people are doing their best. It keeps me out of judgment and lets me focus on what is, and not what should or could be.'

Steve's words gave me a message loud and clear. This is an assumption *I can choose* and that, just as with my friends on Twitter, just as with my colleague who didn't reply to my emails, when I choose to assume it, my life is better. I get a clearer perspective of things, rather than having my view distorted by how I wish things were.

The message of this chapter can feel counterintuitive to our experience of life. Partly, this is because many of us have spent years assuming the opposite: that people are selfish and that our first thoughts about their intentions are correct.

It isn't easy to change something that has been part of us for a long time, so, for many people, it isn't easy to hold onto the assumption that others are doing their best in the practicalities of daily life. This assumption is something that has made my day-to-day life easier and more fulfilling and it has, as Steve said, enabled me to see things more as they are and less as what they should or could be. It has enabled me to leave more experiences feeling happy and satisfied with the way I have responded, rather than wrapped in the stress and regret of 'I should have said X' or 'I wish I hadn't said Y,' both of which used to be incredibly common experiences of mine, but are now rare.

The Train Guard

The practice of *what if everyone is doing their best?* isn't just something that can be done in retrospect or in advance. It can be powerful in the moment; *you can choose* it, even in the heat of an exchange with someone else.

Several years ago, my wife, Emma, and I were travelling back to London by train after visiting her family in the West Midlands.

What If Everyone Is Doing Their Best?

We had paid for Standard Class tickets and had been assigned seat reservations in Coach D. However, when we got on the train, we found that Coach D was the designated First Class carriage[5]. We approached the guard on the platform and asked her what to do, and she told us to find some seats in an alternative carriage. Fine with us.

We calmly settled into some empty seats until, three or four stops later, the train arrived at Oxford. Suddenly, the train became full and an elderly couple approached us with reservations for the very same seats. Of course, we let them sit down. By way of explaining why we were in their seats, we outlined what had happened and the old man suggested going to sit in Coach D, even though it was First Class. "It's their fault," he said.

By this point, the carriage we were in was full and people were even sitting on the floor in the vestibules between carriages, so we took his advice and found two empty seats in Coach D. We were both a bit anxious about this: we didn't have a First Class ticket and so weren't technically allowed to sit there. In the end, our worries came to fruition: the train guard came to check our tickets and explained that we needed to move as we hadn't paid for First Class. His words were polite, but his manner was abrupt.[6]

I could feel my response building in me with a sense of anger and injustice: 'How can he say that to us? We're in this situation because the train company messed up the reservations. And his colleague gave us terrible advice! It always gets busy at Oxford and she should have known that.' Despite my righteous feelings, I really had no idea what was going on for the guard and he knew nothing about what had happened to us. My thinking was moving at a hundred miles an hour and it was moving towards assuming malice, not busyness or incompetence. As Brené Brown's husband said, I was judging the guard and his colleague and I was focused on what *should be*, not what *was*.

I said something first and then Emma started venting her frustration at the guard. As soon as Emma was in the conversation and I was watching, I could see what was happening: both she and the guard were preparing for an argument, getting ready to fight it out until one of them backed down.

Fred Kofman, the academic and leadership consultant whose work I referenced in Chapter One, gives a beautiful demonstration of what happens in situations like this in a video published by Lean In[7]. In the video, which is about how to have difficult conversations, Kofman works with a volunteer from the audience. He asks her to hold her hand up in front of her, palm towards him. He then asks, "If I push…what do you want to do?" and pushes his hand against hers, applying pressure towards her. Her response is immediate: to push back, without the need to even think about it. This is an instinctive reaction most of us have when someone pushes us: it's like closing your eyes if something is dropping into them or moving your hand to bat away an insect from your face. It's a part of being human: if someone pushes us, our instant natural instinctive response is to push back. Not just when someone pushes you physically, but also in relationships and conversations.

Back in Coach D, I caught what was going on. I said, "Just a sec, Emma." I took a breath and took a different point of view: this man is doing his best. If he's doing his best, then, underneath, he wants to help, because that's what a train guard who is doing their best wants and does. He may have been frustrated by us or by other things in his day, and as his frustration pushed up against us, we began to push back[8]. Seeing this from the outside (and through the lens of *what if everyone is doing their best?*), I calmly explained the full sequence of events. He said, still irritably, "You should have come to me before and explained." At this point, I had to pause: he was pushing against me again and my instincts said, clearly and with a physical response in my body, to push back. There were many questions that flew through my mind, sharp words I could have said, but instead I took another breath and chose, again, to ask: *what if everyone is doing their best?*

"We're explaining now," I said, remaining calm. "How can you help?"

It was strange to watch what happened next. He was gearing up for the fight that probably ends up with Emma and I either paying for First Class or standing in the vestibule, fuming and complaining on social media. Instead, I could see him physically relax, switching out of pushing and into something different. He took our tickets and wrote on them 'OK to stay in First Class,' followed by the date and his signature. And there we sat, relaxed, for the rest of the journey.

From that example, I hope that you begin to see what might be possible. There would, of course, have been other ways to deal with this: we might have been able to batter the guard down without that assumption, through arguing or complaining. He might have relented. If we had complained furiously enough to him or someone else, we might have got some money back, or even have got the train guard disciplined by his superiors. But here is why I think this assumption is so important in an ever-more-connected world: those other options, maybe all of them, would have left Emma and I contracted in confrontation mode and they would have left the train guard the same way. The confrontation mode in that case is physical: different chemicals are pumping in our bodies and different parts of our brains are engaged. That's why he relaxed *physically* when I offered him the chance to relent by asking the question. He was shifting out of some version of the fight/flight/freeze response.[9]

When you think about confrontations or disagreements, or put yourself in my position with the train guard, you may ask 'Why should it be my responsibility to do this, to take a breath and take responsibility?' or 'Why is it me and not the train guard who needs to do this?' Well, the world would be a wonderful place if everyone was nimble enough in every moment to shift a conversation away from unnecessary confrontation and vitriol, but none of us can do this all of the time. Even when both people are aware of the possibility of making a shift like this, it won't always happen. Each and every one of us sometimes gets carried away by our instinctive reactions. That's part of being a human, with a brain that evolved for a simpler time, facing the complexity of today's world. So, when you *can* make the shift, when you have the awareness and agility in the moment, do it. Do it because, in all the ways I shared at the start of the chapter, our interactions with others colour our days. If we have the skill and grace to handle a conversation with a frazzled train guard well, he is more likely to do the same later for other customers, or when he goes home to his family at the end of the day, having had one fewer unpleasant interaction and one more positive resolution. We can let judgment, resentment and anger ripple out or we can let connection, kindness and possibility ripple out.

We can choose.

And that's how we change the world, one interaction at a time.

Away from the Scarcity of 'I'm Right and They're Wrong'

If we had argued with the train guard, he might have changed his position. Or maybe he would have pushed back furiously as we pushed at him, digging his heels in and stubbornly sticking to the point. He would have been right that we didn't have a ticket for First Class, but Emma and I were right that the situation was confusing and difficult, *and* he was probably right that it would have been better to speak to him earlier, *and* we were probably right that his colleague could have given us better advice. Being right about those things didn't solve our problems or his, though. Instead, by stepping back from the confrontation and the sense of scarcity that comes from 'I'm right and they're wrong' or 'only one of us can be right here,' we stepped into possibility. We did that through the assumption of *what if everyone is doing their best?* It allowed us to reach a conclusion that both he and we were happy with and it allowed all of us to leave the situation feeling connected, in touch with each other and in touch with the higher parts of ourselves.

Pursuing an argument to 'win' the situation is a game *you can choose* not to play. It's a game for the baser part of you or for older parts that are no longer useful. It's a game for the child in you who lost and was embarrassed, humiliated and scared, who is still a part of you and wants to win *now* to heal the wounds of the past. I can tell you that it won't heal the past. You might feel better for a few minutes, you might get what you want on the outside, but you will still 'need' to win next time. When the baser parts of you rest again later in the day and the higher parts of you come back online, you might find yourself regretting how you 'won.'

By choosing not to play the 'winning and losing' game, there is an opportunity to step into your Higher Self, to step beyond those difficult times from your past and do something different, something good for yourself and others. Win together by assuming that the other person is doing their best.

The Dance

The truly remarkable thing about this practice is how often and how fast the behaviour of someone else changes when you change how *you* are and don't even tell them what you are doing. That's what happened with the train guard and I have seen it happen with clients, friends, shop assistants and, as I'll explain in Chapter Five, my wife.

One client who saw the change happen quickly was an entrepreneur a few years into a new business venture. Improving the client's relationship with his founding business partner, which was fundamental to the functioning and future success of the business, was part of our work. In one session, as this came up, I shared the idea of *what if everyone is doing their best?* For the client, it landed best through the practice from *The Art of Possibility*: 'What if I gave him an A? What if my business partner is not only doing his best, but what if I assume that he is doing his best to a standard that deserves a Grade A?'

Almost straight away, the client saw how he was *not* giving his colleague an A. He found himself reading an email from his business partner with another member of their team and suddenly caught not only himself but also the team member assigning Grade C (at best) motives to the business partner. My client was able to catch this, taking a breath as I did with the train guard, and read the email again from a different point of view. What happened over the next few weeks was spectacular: the client took a strong commitment to assign only Grade A motives and to listen for and acknowledge those motives carefully in his conversations. This took concentration and commitment, often ignoring how things had initially come across (in person or in writing) in favour of that assumption.

The improvement in the relationship was as big as it was swift: over a matter of days my client observed dozens of interactions that might have previously gone down the road of conflict. Instead, these conversations were productive and the relationship between the two partners was strengthened: they were able to trust each other more, be more assertive and even be more honest in their defensiveness with each other when they felt it, without the relationship suffering and without resentment being carried into other areas of their work and lives. As the quality of their conversations became more productive, both were able to assume more secure and well-defined roles in the organisation. The business results, which relied on both their strengths, soon followed.

This kind of change is precisely what happens next in Fred Kofman's video about difficult conversations. After demonstrating the principle of how we push back when we are pushed, Kofman explains what happens if you do something different: if you can catch yourself pushing back and choose to behave differently, possibilities emerge. Kofman invites us to assume that if someone pushes against us in a conversation, they may be seeing something we don't; he invites us to give them the benefit of the doubt. To demonstrate this, he moves with the woman's push and they begin to move together, turning to see things from different angles. Kofman is Argentinian and they move into a tango. This is what I was able to do in those moments with the train guard, thanks to the assumption *what if everyone is doing their best?* And this is what my client was able to do with his business partner with a conscious shift of emphasis in emails and meetings. By giving his business partner the benefit of the doubt instead of pushing back against him, they moved into the dance.

Are You Sure?

The process of shifting our perspectives isn't always easy. The idea *what if everyone is doing their best?* and, underneath that, the assertion that people's motivations may be different from what we initially assume, can be hard to grasp. Our behaviour and our thoughts can be settled, stationary and final, built up over many years of a certain way of seeing someone or something. The way through these assumptions lies in the seed of doubt, in the idea that there is even the smallest possibility that the certainty we feel may be what is holding us back. When we can see that seed of doubt and reduce our certainty, we get the chance to do the developmental move we touched on earlier: to take the certainty we have previously had, transcend it and include it in a new, more complexity-fit way of seeing the world.

The following piece of writing, by my father, Pete Armstrong, was instrumental in giving me the gift of less certainty. The question that exposes this lack of certainty, sows the seed of doubt and opens up possibility is the title of the piece: are you sure? It speaks to those times when we are *sure* our assumption is correct, stationary and final, and to the necessity of the seed of doubt.

Are You Sure? by Pete Armstrong[10]

> If you are a car driver you may have experienced certain behaviours from other drivers, and learned to label them.
>
> For example you may be driving along a rural A road and come up behind a steady stream of traffic. The road is single carriage-way and winding. Overtaking is not a safe option, and you settle back to be part of a convoy until the nature of the road changes.
>
> However the driver who comes up behind you does not, apparently, see the situation in the same way. He is hanging on your tail and edging out into the road looking for a chance to shoot past you. You may well feel uncomfortably tense at his behaviour and notice other feelings and responses starting to rise in you.

What If Everyone Is Doing Their Best?

You may well therefore feel relief when, at an opportune moment, he accelerates past you and pulls into the gap ahead. Because you are a careful driver, the gap ahead of you is quite large. However, the same is not true of all the cars ahead, and as you watch the driver make his hurried way up through the convoy, you see lots of sudden red brake lights as the car pulls into narrow gaps to avoid oncoming traffic.

If all the drivers were connected by radio, no doubt the airwaves would be full of complaints and invective: 'stupid risk-taking', 'dangerous driving,' 'all BMW drivers are the same,' 'where are the police when you need them?' 'he's going to die soon in a head-on, and he'll deserve it.'

Perhaps most of the time, the driver in question would respond in similar vein: 'get out of my way, losers,' 'it's a free country, I'll do what I like,' 'if you all drove like me, life would be more exciting,' 'all you little people, get back to your hovels and stop cluttering up the roads.'

But can you be certain what the response would be? Perhaps, just occasionally, you might hear the driver say something like, 'I'm very sorry, but can you let me through? I've just heard my mother is dying in hospital, and I must get to her.'

In situations where critical judgment seems called for, you may like to ask yourself: am I sure?

Maybe, in the absence of radios, giving someone the benefit of the doubt is the correct choice.

It is hard for me not to think that my dad's normal, careful driving might have given way to weaving in and out of traffic in the moment he found out his mother was dying. It's hard not to imagine that mine might, too. And that for either of us, or someone else, it would be understandable even if not advisable.

What if everyone is doing their best? allows us a way to shift in the moments when the sense of 'uncomfortable tension' rises. It's the same if someone pushes in front of us in the queue at the supermarket or bashes us out of the way as they race for the train or down the street. Tension rises and our quality of thinking falls. We are swept into the pushing match of Kofman's demonstration, sometimes with someone who, by that point, is out of sight, but who we hold onto through our tense and contracted reaction. Then, locked in this imaginary pushing match, our decision-making ability and our thinking get worse. In a station or on the street, perhaps this doesn't matter so much. In a car, hurtling along the road at 60mph, having our thinking clouded is mighty risky. And what about when you are having a meeting with a colleague or a manager while your thinking is still polluted by the dangerous driver? Or what about when it's your wife or boyfriend or child whose behaviour has you locked in a sense of uncomfortable tension? If there was a shortcut out of that, to clearer and more effective thinking, wouldn't you want to take it?

That shortcut is in the seed of doubt: are you sure? And it is in the question: what if this person is doing their best?

We all have these contractions, these animal- or child-like behaviours, when we feel under threat. These are wrapped up in our Deeper Selves from our evolutionary history and our childhood experiences. We all have these moments when someone pushes against us and we push back. Am I sure? What if I had been through what they have? What would I have to go through to be where they are? It might have taken more than they have been through for you to do something like weave dangerously through traffic, or it might have taken less. It may be a story the same as theirs, or it may be different. But *are you sure* they don't have a good reason?

If this was the best they could do in this situation, what might they have been through for that to be true? If you shift to this perspective, what changes for you? What do you see differently?

Where Do We Draw Our Boundaries?

So far, I have outlined how the key assumption of this chapter helps us to release tension and contraction in interactions with others, improving our ability to read situations, increasing our chances of good outcomes, and removing stress from our lives. In the final parts of this chapter, it's important to address this question: if everyone is doing their best, where do we draw the line of what behaviour is acceptable and what isn't?

The first assumption that almost everyone seems to make when confronted with *what if everyone is doing their best?* is something like: 'If everyone is a human doing their best, then their behaviour is excused.' In other words, 'If they're doing their best, does that mean I have to let them get away with whatever they want?'

In my experience, the opposite has been true.

Yes, in some circumstances, *what if everyone is doing their best?* has allowed me to quickly release and forgive behaviour: the speeding car, the man jumping the queue, the woman pushing past me on the platform. In others, it has empowered me to stand up for what I believe in more confidently and clearly than before. More than that, when I use this assumption, I am more confident that I am helping someone else see things differently than when I might confront or challenge them without that assumption: this goes back to Kofman and the dance.

The first step is to think about how and when we draw those lines, our boundaries, with the behaviour of others.

I would love to give hard and fast rules for this, but, unfortunately, I have discovered through years of working with clients and thinking about it that trying to define rules for something like this would be a fool's errand. No matter how sophisticated I think I might be in drawing up those rules, they wouldn't be fit for the complexity of our world. Even seemingly straightforward rules for challenging others look clumsy in the face of the shades of grey of real life.

That really only leaves us with one choice: it has to be an exercise for each of us to understand when and where to draw our lines and boundaries, to individually choose when to challenge or confront someone.

To decide when to draw lines with others as your Higher Self, you first need the assumption of this chapter to help you shift out of judgment with the other, and see things more how they are, and less as you wish they were.

Then, you need to reflect on what is most important *to you*. Once you know what matters deeply to you, *you can choose* to honour it. That is the guide we need to help us understand whether someone has crossed the line of what is acceptable to us with their behaviour.

There are many ways to do this work to understand what matters deeply to you. You can start by simply asking yourself, in a moment when you feel calm and clear: 'What values are central to who I am?' The answers might come back as concepts, feelings, behaviours or in other forms that are specific to you. Another powerful way to understand this is to consider the things that would make you sad at the end of your life: how would you have been or not been, what would you have done or not done, that would leave you with sadness on your deathbed? Another valuable data set is to notice when you are frustrated or upset by others. What about their behaviour is upsetting you? Could it be that they are violating one of the things that matters deeply to you? With the answers to questions and reflections like these, we can see more clearly where our Higher Selves might choose to draw the line.

In the cold light of day, there is no better fast-track to do this that I know of than The Honour Question I outlined in Chapter One: what would I have to do in this situation so that, regardless of the outcomes, I will feel at peace with myself? This is a shortcut to our values, to us on our best days, to our Higher Selves.

Sometimes, the answer will come back: I need to speak up and challenge this behaviour; I won't be at peace if I let this slide. Sometimes challenging someone else's behaviour won't be part of the answer at all, even when I expect it to be.

We can use The Honour Question retrospectively, too, when we know we haven't lived up to our Higher Selves: what would I have needed to do to be at peace with myself? What do I wish I'd done? The answer becomes our recipe for next time.

Through understanding your values and using The Honour Question, you can begin to get clearer on where you will draw your personal lines, where you will stand up to others. This isn't the end of the journey, but it does open up space so that *you can choose*. Am I going to act in line with my instincts and past behaviour, or am I going to choose to honour this value that is central to who I am? Each time we make this conscious by thinking through a situation actively, and act to draw a line with someone, we code it into our intuition. If we're not used to challenging others, it will feel weird at first and we'll need to practise until it becomes gradually easier.

We can use these ideas to help us stand up in the moments when our values call us to do it, and draw a boundary, especially whilst holding to the assumption that the other person is doing their best.

With *what if everyone is doing their best?* in mind, you will probably find that the drawing of boundaries is much smoother and is received far more generously than you would have imagined.

What Does It Mean to Be Doing Our Best?

Because we are humans, sometimes we won't act in line with what matters most to us, no matter how much we have thought about it.

Sometimes you will slip out of your Higher Self, away from those values, because of the unconscious patterns and instincts contained in the deeper parts of you.

With all this in mind, we might then define 'doing our best' as: dancing the dance between the unconscious patterns and instincts in our Deeper Selves and the possibilities of our Higher Selves. This definition of 'doing our best' and our knowledge of how hard the dance can be can often be enough to give us compassion for someone who seems to be struggling to live as their Higher Self.

For many of us, perhaps even most of us, we largely live in ignorance of the patterns and instincts that govern our behaviour. I certainly did, until the involuntary stop I spoke about in the introduction woke me up and showed me something different. Once we know that this is happening, that our childhood patterns and evolutionary instincts affect us so much, there is an imperative to step up to do the work to understand your Deeper Self. Only by continually doing that work, which we will speak more about in Chapter Three, can you make the dance with those instincts easier, and give yourself more access to the skilful, wise, honourable Higher Self. That's how we build our capacity, as individuals and societies, to respond to complex challenges. Once we become aware of how important the unconscious parts of us are, only by doing that work can we really *know* that we are doing our best.

It can be tempting to see the core idea of this chapter as naïve, to believe that given 'how people actually are' in the real world, it will just lead to our exploitation. Whilst I imagine it's true that a genuinely bad actor might twist our assumption and take advantage of us giving the benefit of the doubt, that won't be the case for almost all the interactions in almost all of our lives. I have sat in conversation with many, many people and I have heard their answers when I ask what is most important to them and why. Those answers are heart-warming and inspiring: each time I dig into what matters most with a client, I have found deep goodness. That is what gives me confidence that if more of us act through the lens of *what if everyone is doing their best?*, we will tilt our lives and the wider world in the right direction far more than we will be exploited.

Should one of us be faced with someone genuinely malevolent, or with such a different brain make-up that they might be classed by some psychologists as having a personality disorder, my feeling is that this assumption would continue, even then, to empower us to make the right decisions. If this person's manipulative behaviour is the best they can do, then what do I need to do here?

It shifts us away from how we want things to be – the damaging presence in our life behaving honourably, perhaps – and closer to reality: that the difficult line we haven't wanted to draw with them must be drawn, for our good or theirs or both.

What if everyone is doing their best? can be an exercise in deep compassion and in understanding of the human condition: through it, you may come to understand what other people might have been through in order to do the things that look unpleasant (or malevolent) to us as outsiders. As we continually do this, stretching ourselves to understand what others may have been through in order to do these things, we will sometimes see more clearly the ways that we, too, are victims of the patterns and beliefs and assumptions inside us.

The scars humans take away from their interactions with each other can create the patterns and instincts of our Deeper Selves, which we then have to work with, transcend and include to do our best. That makes it particularly important to be sure that we are doing the work to be as skilful and noble as we can in the moments when we are relating to others. If we are going to call someone's behaviour into question, to decide a certain behaviour is unacceptable to us, to stand up for our values against someone else, we need to do what we can not to add to the scars and patterns that they carry, not to make things worse. If we must challenge someone, we need to challenge them in a way that encourages them to do the work so that they will do better tomorrow than they did today. This takes us to the final part of this chapter: the distinction between guilt and shame.

Guilt and Shame

Some form of confrontation will continue to exist for all of us, even as we learn to act more and more as our Higher Selves[11]. Values of care, respect, integrity, honesty and more may challenge us to maintain our boundaries. If this is the case, we may find ourselves drawing a line like this: 'Look, I know you are doing your best. I know something has led you here and I believe you are trying to act from your innate goodness. But this behaviour is hurting me, it is hurting you and it is hurting others and it has to stop. And if it doesn't stop, then there are consequences.'

Brené Brown spoke about this at the talk I attended in November 2015. She described the example of a friend who drinks too much. Most of us can probably relate to this: someone who has been through a tough time, perhaps, or who is struggling with their life in some way, whose ability to control their drinking has slipped. They may embarrass you and upset you, or they may even upset or hurt someone you know, but you mostly forgive them because you

What If Everyone Is Doing Their Best?

know things have been hard and they are doing their best. I have seen people drinking and behaving like this, and I have undoubtedly done it myself, too. Often, forgiveness here is warranted and noble, but there may come a point where you have to say to your friend, for their good, for your good or for the good of others, 'No, you have to stop now. This is too far. That is the boundary.' Perhaps to say something like what Brown said to her friend. It might be: 'I can be here for you, I can look after you, I can try to help you through this, but I can't have you in my house, drunk like this, when others are here. It is hurting me and it is hurting others.'

This brings us to the crucial distinction between guilt and shame. As a simple working definition, borrowed from Brown's work, guilt is 'you *did* bad, I *did* bad.' Shame is 'you *are* bad, I *am* bad.' This may seem a small difference, but it is significant: there is almost no way back from 'I am bad.' This is how I *am*. Fixed. Forever. But from 'I did bad,' there is the possibility to change.

Brown talks about shame as an epidemic in our societies. Shame is the story that keeps us trapped, keeps us contracted and keeps us away from a sense of possibility for ourselves and others. Shame stops us from reaching or even acknowledging that we have a Higher Self. Instead, we are left with the terribly permanent assumption that 'I am bad.' From the seeming permanence of shame comes a story that I can't possibly be a good person, ever. To a greater or lesser extent, this is the story that we tell others when we blame, punish and hold our boundaries without the belief that 'this person is doing their best.' However, when we use our new assumption, stopping someone at our boundary with 'I believe you are doing your best' behind what we say, we are not telling them that they *are* bad. We are telling them that, deep down, we believe they are good and doing the best they can in the moment. They are dancing the dance between their Deeper Self and Higher Self. This time, though, we see that they *did* bad. This gives them the opportunity to change. This gives them 'next time, things can be different.'

What if everyone is doing their best? almost always enhances our judgment of others, making it clearer and more grounded in reality. In the case of my colleague earlier in the chapter, clearer judgment might lead us to conclude that failing to organise your emails is not acceptable in an organisation, especially if it leads, say, to financial costs. We might decide that some of the 'jokes' my friends made to me on Twitter were offensive, uncalled for or cruel. We certainly might decide that speeding through traffic in a dangerous way is beyond the line of what is acceptable, whatever the intention and reasoning of the driver.

Importantly, *what if everyone is doing their best?* shifts us into judging what these people *did* and not who they *are*. It helps us be clearer and less tense as we say what might be a difficult thing to someone we may care about, and it allows us to treat people with the honour and understanding that we ourselves would want to be given.

There are times in life when your ability to challenge someone's behaviour skilfully – so skilfully that they might change their behaviour in future – will make a big difference in your life or the lives of others. It will take courage, but the assumption of this chapter will help you be brave. As you do these things from the assumption *what if everyone is doing their best?*, you will increase the likelihood that you can express clearly and correctly the challenge you are making *and* you will increase the likelihood that the person you are speaking to hears you and changes, because you are speaking to their behaviour and not their sense of self.

Through your courage, the courage to believe the best in others, to give them the benefit of the doubt, your relationships will be transformed.

How Do I Do This?

This whole chapter is about understanding the perspectives of others. It is a practice; it's something you have to do repeatedly to give yourself the nimbleness to respond in the moment. Sometimes, if you just remind yourself of this idea, when frustrated with slow service in a coffee shop or when someone pushes in front of you in a queue, your experience of the situation will shift for you and you will be able to respond more skilfully and get the results you want. If you pause before you send an email, you may think: 'Ah, I'm giving this person a Grade C here. How would I get this same point across to them if they were a Grade A colleague?' If you do this, you may notice that they respond more as a Grade A colleague, and less as a Grade C colleague.

Sometimes, it takes more thought. A long-standing, particularly tangled relationship may take significantly more reflection. If you need to, take some time to write out how it might be possible that someone is doing their best or ask someone else to help you see it, especially if your attitudes to this person have been the same for a long time. Sit down and ask the questions that are in this chapter; this can be done after an event to work through frustration and it can be done in advance of a conversation you know you will find difficult. Work your curiosity. How could this person, even in this moment where I am left frustrated or upset, be doing their best? When faced with someone who has done something that you think is unacceptable, something that makes you furious or frustrated or upset, ask: what would it take for me to behave in this way?

Find the answer. Because you could behave in that way. You know you could, if circumstances were different, or if your day had started a certain way, or if your life had started a certain way. If you really can't imagine yourself in that situation, ask what it would take for your husband to behave like that, or your mother, or your son.

So much of our life is circumstance. The place and time we were born, the education system we were part of, the friends we make. The Human Genome Project has reported that all humans are 99.9% genetically identical. We are all so similar to everyone on the planet. Almost always, it could be us.

Sometimes, we need to understand the bigger, longer-term picture of how someone may be doing their best. Their upbringing, their education, the things they have been through in their formative years. For the most part, however, it's easier than that. We can imagine being the irritable train guard, or an obstructive colleague, or a person making a joke that is hurtful to someone else, because we have at times behaved in a similar way ourselves (if we are honest). We can then reflect on what it would take for us to behave in that way again.

We don't always need to forgive people for the things they have done, although often we may choose to, but by choosing the key assumption of this chapter, we will see things more clearly. With that clarity, we will act more wisely not to make things worse and we will act more skilfully to make things better.

To make this shift, you need to work your curiosity muscles on other people. The questions you need are scattered throughout this chapter and outlined in the summary below: what would it take for them to behave like this? How did they get here? If I got here, or my sister got here, or my father, or my spouse, how would I want them to be helped or spoken to? At the centre of these questions is: *what if everyone is doing their best?*

Start small. Experiment. See what happens.

Even for someone like me, who was lucky to have this principle implicitly present in their upbringing, it was only when *what if everyone is doing their best?* had been brought to light for me several

What If Everyone Is Doing Their Best?

times in my adult life that I started to make it a bedrock of who I am, actively practising it whenever I could. Even then, I still slip up and take wrong turns, and it needs ongoing work and reminders so that *I can choose* to come back to the path of *what if everyone is doing their best?* As with all change, just seeing the insight isn't enough. You have to apply it every day.

I have seen increasingly clearly that there is no long-term fulfilment in 'winning' in conversations, in shaming or resenting people, all of which used to be far more common in my way of being. Those things don't help me and don't make me feel good, even though my baser instincts try to persuade me otherwise. Life is about more than the short-term rush, or at least it is if you choose the adventure I am inviting you on. Life, instead, can be about making the world a better place when you leave than it was when you arrived and living like that every day. 'Beating' people, resenting and shaming won't change others for the better. These things will just add to the complex and tangled patterns and stories that get between them and their Higher Self. On the journey to creating a world with all of us living more as our Higher Selves, more able to respond skilfully to the complex challenges the world may present, it is up to each of us to send out ripples of connection, kindness and goodwill, and not ripples of anger, vindictiveness and pain.

In any moment, you can change the relationship you have with someone. You can probably change the way they feel and you can certainly change the way you feel. This chapter and, indeed, this whole book, is about helping you to make that shift, from tension and contraction to skill, wisdom and nobility. *You can choose* how you feel about the people around you. In choosing to assume that they are doing their best, you will find yourself moving from scarcity and resentment to possibility and your Higher Self.

CHAPTER TWO SUMMARY

Key idea: Our relationships with others will be improved if we choose to live through the question: *what if everyone is doing their best?* When we choose to assume this, we shift out of judgment and see the world as it is, not as we think it ought to be.

Exercises, practices and questions for reflection:

- **What if this person is doing their best?** Ask yourself this when you find yourself frustrated or angry or upset with someone. Practise it when your interactions leave you a bitter taste or you feel like a victim. Notice what changes with this question.

- **If this person deserves an A for their performance in this relationship, why might that be?** What reasons can you find to give them an A? How could their behaviour actually be Grade A behaviour?

- **Am I sure?** How might I be wrong? If I have a little more doubt and a little less certainty, what can I see about this person that I couldn't see before?

- **Do work to understand what matters deeply to you.** Start by simply asking yourself, in a moment when you feel calm and clear: 'What values are central to who I am?' The answers might come back as concepts, feelings, behaviours or in other forms that are specific to you. Consider the things that would make you sad at the end of your life: how would you have been or not been, what would you have done or not done, that would leave you with sadness on your deathbed? Notice when in life you are frustrated or upset by others: what about their behaviour is upsetting you? Could it be that they are violating one of the things that matters deeply to you?

- **Fast-track to knowing what to do in a situation by using The Honour Question.** What would I have to do in this situation so that, regardless of the outcomes, I will feel at peace with myself? You can use it retrospectively, too, when you know you haven't lived up to the ideals of your Higher Self: what would I have needed to do to be at peace with myself? The answer then becomes your recipe for next time.

- **Take some time to write out the answer to 'How could this person be doing their best?' for a long-standing or particularly tangled relationship.** If you need to, ask someone else to help, especially if your attitudes to the person have been the same for a long time. Again, notice: what happened when you got some answers to the question 'How could this person be doing their best?' What difference did it make to your interactions, your conversations and the way you experience life?

- **What would it take for me to behave in this way?** What would I have to have gone through to do what they are doing? If what the person has done was the best they could do in this situation, what might they have been through for that to be true? What does this shift in perspective change for you? If I found myself here, or my brother/mother/partner, how would I want them to be helped?

Further Reading and Learning

- *The Art of Possibility* by Rosamund Stone Zander and Benjamin Zander

- *Rising Strong* by Brené Brown

- *Difficult Conversations* with Fred Kofman: www.youtube.com/watch?v=_TNrSo1brdY. For further reading by Kofman, I recommend his book, *The Meaning Revolution*.

- *Follow the Lady with the Pink Parasol Along the Winding Path* by Pete Armstrong

CHAPTER THREE

CURIOSITY IS THE ANTIDOTE TO CONTRACTION

If there is one single attribute that we need in order to create the shifts that will lead us towards our skilful, wise, noble Higher Self, it is curiosity.

In Chapter One, I explained that *you can choose* from different sets of beliefs and assumptions far more than you think. To do that, you need to engage your curiosity about the ways you are thinking: what am I assuming here? What else could I choose to believe or think? Which choice would best enable me to live life as my Higher Self in this moment, to respond skilfully to the complex challenges I am facing? In Chapter Two, I asked you to work your curiosity with the people around you, asking *what if everyone is doing their best?* Getting curious about the perspectives of others enables us to step out of judgment, see things more clearly and live more as our Higher Selves in our relationships with other people.

In this chapter, I will ask you to turn your curiosity on yourself again. Not directly on your thinking, however. Through the key idea of this chapter – *curiosity is the antidote to contraction* – I will invite you to delve into your Deeper Self, the less conscious parts of you that often govern your behaviour, whether they come from your genes or your life experience. When we do this, we give ourselves a greater opportunity to choose not to act on these evolutionary or learned instincts. If we want to live more as our Higher Selves, then it is vital in the long run to be courageous enough to look deeply at our experience of life. More than that, our stresses and anxieties are often entangled with our Deeper Selves. By doing the work in this chapter, we can significantly reduce their impact on our day-to-day experience. We can reduce our stress, increase our skill, become more adept at dealing with the complexity of the world and contribute more fully.

The work of this chapter is to untangle the patterns that hold us back, that leave us contracted. Curiosity is the path to understanding our Deeper Selves. By understanding our Deeper Selves, we can see the traps that we fall into more often. Once we see these traps, *we can choose* to make the choices of our Higher Selves.

The Opposite of Contraction Isn't Openness

Around the time of the break-up I described in the introduction, my brother, writer and coach, Ewan Townhead, sent me a recording. It was of a conversation he had had with Guy Sengstock, a facilitator and philosopher, and one of the founders of Circling, a relational practice that supports people to develop authentic connection with others. Ewan sent me the conversation in part out of sympathy and a desire to connect with me at a time when I needed it. He asked me for feedback, although as far as I know the recording never saw the light of day, but it certainly had an impact on me.

The language we have available to us affects our ability to describe our own experience; once we can describe something that is going on for us, we can separate it from ourselves and take perspective on it. As I have discussed already, once we can take perspective on something, then *we can choose.* The conversation between Ewan and Guy opened up important language for me as I grappled with a set of circumstances for which I didn't have the skills.

One of the terms that Ewan and Guy introduced me to was 'triggered.' At the time, this term wasn't used much outside of psychology textbooks and therapy rooms. Now, it has become far more commonplace, so much so that for many readers it may not require a definition. In the world of psychology, however, it has a very specific meaning: something – often a sight, a sound or a smell – that brings back feelings of trauma. This might apply, for instance, to someone suffering from Post-Traumatic Stress Disorder (PTSD).

Today, that meaning has expanded as its use in broader society has increased. For the purposes of this book, I will use this definition: being triggered is when something in our life brings a difficult[1] historical experience we have had into the present. Even if we haven't experienced the kind of deep trauma a psychologist might work with, each of us has had difficult experiences, particularly as a child or adolescent. We also all have a set of evolutionary responses, such as the commonly discussed fight/flight/freeze response to danger. Because of those difficult experiences and our evolutionary responses, there are times when we slip into a different state, the stimulus in the world seeming to lead directly to a change inside us (although, for most of us, it will thankfully never be the extreme reaction of someone suffering from PTSD).

Guy and Ewan also used another word: 'contraction.' This was a word that, in this context, was new to me, too, but with the gift of the language to describe it, I began to notice the 'contraction' feeling in myself: it was happening all the time in the aftermath of the break-up. This is the state I described in Chapter Two when I couldn't sleep after the Twitter spat with my friends: a feeling of breath changing, mood changing, sometimes our whole physiology changing as a response to something that has happened. For me, contraction is a feeling of tightness in the chest, almost as if my shoulders are being folded in on themselves, squashing my heart in between (it feels like my body is literally contracting). It can be a state of fight or flight or, more often for me, freeze. In that final case, I simply can't react. I don't know what to do. It can be frightening. As I engaged my curiosity on these experiences, I came to see that this state is almost always a historical response, sometimes an evolutionary one and sometimes from my past. It is not a place in which I want to spend time; it is certainly not a place that allows me to be my Higher Self.

I had to listen to the recording of Ewan and Guy several times to grasp these new concepts and begin to integrate them into my experience of the world. Sometimes it takes a long time to learn something that changes your perspective. It may take a whole book, read slowly and then applied over weeks or months. It may take three different people sharing the same thing with you in different ways. That's what happened for me with the principle *what if everyone is doing their best?* I had years of that idea popping up or being shown to me, but only at the Brené Brown talk did it finally fall into place. At other times, it takes just one moment of insight, combined with a chance to immediately put the idea into practice. That moment arrived in the recording when Guy said: "The opposite of contraction isn't openness. It's curiosity." And then: "Curiosity is the opposite of contraction."

As you will come to see, this idea has evolved into a tool I have used in my most difficult moments ever since.

Before we get to that, we need to distinguish between states and processes. A *state* of openness actually is, in my experience and maybe yours, a pretty good description for the opposite of the *state* of being contracted. So, if we are feeling contracted, then it seems

Curiosity Is the Antidote to Contraction

sensible to wish for openness, to strive for it. Unfortunately, striving for openness is a little like striving for calm when you are panicked, or trying to clear your mind by putting in more effort ('Meditate harder, you fool!' says my internal voice, definitively not helping me meditate). Note again that openness is the opposite of the *state of being contracted* (or at least a good approximation for it). *Contraction*, however, is a noun that means 'the process of becoming smaller.' The question is then: what, on a psychological level, helps slow or stop the process of becoming smaller? What helps us with the process of becoming bigger? A powerful answer, in my experience and that of Ewan, Guy, many of my clients and many others (some of whose work I will discuss in this chapter), is curiosity.

Curiosity is the kryptonite for contraction. Curiosity is the equal and opposite force to contraction. If you're contracting, it won't help you reverse that process to think of openness (no matter how hard you think). In fact, my experience is often that I can't even remember what the state of openness is like when I'm in that contracted state; it feels a long, long way away. What you need in those moments is a force to help you, something that will slow and then reverse the effects of contraction. You need an antidote, and *curiosity is the antidote to contraction*. Through curiosity, you will find the path to your Higher Self: the bigger version of you, transcending and including your previous ways of seeing the world with the new insight you have discovered through your curiosity.

First, curiosity can help in the moment, giving you a way to shift out of your contraction. Secondly, curiosity will take you on a longer-term journey to learning more about yourself through your most difficult moments, gradually opening up your patterns to reveal deeper parts of yourself. Each time, it will help you be nimbler in the dance with those parts of you: enabling you to live more as your Higher Self.

Recently, I learned more about the neuroscience of what is happening when we engage our curiosity in the face of contraction. *The Science and Psychology of Polarisation*, a 2019 series from the YouTube channel, Rebel Wisdom, focuses heavily on the work of neuroscientist, Steven Porges, and clinical psychologist, Peter Levine[2]. Porges developed what is known as Polyvagal Theory, focused on the vagus nerve, which is the longest nerve in the body and connects all the major organs and the face, voice and ears. Porges explains: "Polyvagal Theory emphasises that under challenge, under demands that could be illness or threat, our autonomic nervous system shifts state. It moves from this social engagement safe state, where we are connected to others, to defensive states." These defensive states include the fight, flight, and freeze responses – Porges' work significantly contributed to our understanding of the freeze response. These defensive responses often happen when we find ourselves in a contraction: the state of our nervous system has changed.

Levine has worked as a clinical psychologist in the field of stress and trauma for over 40 years, developing a body-oriented approach called Somatic Experiencing. This work was done independently of Porges' research, but when they discovered each other's conclusions, they realised that their work supported each other's theories and practice.

"You can't be curious and traumatised at the same time," says Levine. "The physiology doesn't allow them to both be there." This is because we can only be curious when we are in the social engagement state that Porges described, not when we feel under threat. Not only can we not be curious and be in our defensive states at the same time, but it would also seem that we are not even able to take on new information when under threat.

"If you can enlist the client in being curious about their sensations and images and feelings," Levine continues, discussing how to

Curiosity Is the Antidote to Contraction

support people who find themselves in those defensive states, "then you've gotten half-way there."

Curiosity, you might say, is the antidote to those feelings of threat.

As I heard the phrase 'curiosity is the opposite of contraction' from Guy in the recording and as he and Ewan explored ideas around it, the concept slipped into my consciousness. At the time, I desperately needed something to help me: I had tried everything else and things were not going well. I had been living in contraction: thoughts, ideas and reminders triggered me into that state, taking me back into grief for the lost relationship, the lost future that I had imagined and other difficult experiences from further back in my past. I was wrapped in guilt for who I had been and fear that I didn't know who I would be next. I resented people around me who I felt had let me down and I was resentful of the loneliness I felt at losing them. I physically moved myself away to a different town. Getting away did allow me to insulate myself from at least some of the reactions I was having, but still the reminders were everywhere, trigger after trigger, contraction after contraction.

Some things made a difference – developing my understanding through conversation, ideas and learning helped – but still the contractions came, and I felt helpless, lost and adrift. I was desperate to feel better and, although I couldn't see it clearly at the time, the 'better' that I wanted was a feeling of control and agency in my life. I wanted to find my way back to a place where *I could choose*. That, in the end, was what arrived through the key idea of this chapter.

Here's something I've come to believe: time doesn't, in fact, heal. I think it's perfectly possible to sit, ignoring a problem, ignoring an unresolved part of your story for many years without anything shifting and without feeling any better at all. If we genuinely want to heal our mental or emotional selves, I think that what we need is more understanding, not more time to pass, and understanding comes from curiosity.

Guy's idea that curiosity is the opposite of contraction gave me the power to act in the moments when I found myself contracting. It gave me something to do when I felt helpless, and that something worked. It gave me a way to deal with what was coming up for me, to take control of my situation. It gave me an antidote to my contraction and to my hopelessness. It is an antidote I have used ever since, taking back control of my life in moments of hopelessness, remembering that I am not a victim in my life: I am a creator.

It's Not About the Chicken

I've heard that Fred Kofman tells a story that goes something like this.

He was having dinner in a small restaurant. As dinner went on, he became aware of a couple sitting a few tables away, engaged in some kind of disagreement. The size of the restaurant meant that he and the other diners gradually picked up on the tension between the couple. A few minutes later, the disagreement came to a head just as conversation in the restaurant quieted. The woman looked up at the man and said: 'It's not about the chicken, Harry. It's about the last 20 years.'

This is what is happening for us when we get triggered and find ourselves contracting. In the present moment, we feel pain or contraction, but the pain and contraction are almost never about what they first appear: it's almost never about the chicken.

Ros Zander, in her 2016 book, *Pathways to Possibility*, writes about how our strong emotional reactions can be viewed as memories. What happens is what our definition of 'triggered' from earlier in the chapter says: something in the world in the present brings back a difficult, historical experience from our memory, just like a sight, sound or smell may for someone suffering from PTSD.

Zander speaks from her experience as a family therapist, using clients' examples to demonstrate that these contractions are memories from our childhood, when life was much scarier and more outside our control. When our behaviour comes from these memories, we are much more childlike, without the mature clarity of the Higher Self. Curiosity in the face of these memories and contractions can teach us about ourselves and our upbringing. It can show us how and why we developed our patterns and behaviours and allow us to integrate them into our adult selves with compassion. We can look at these contractions, then, and see them as a memory rather than a fact about our present circumstances. The perspective we can gain from seeing them in this way can give us more space to respond. Sometimes this means *we can choose* in the present not to act or think in the way the memory would otherwise take us.

We can also be taken even further back, triggered and contracting into the ancient evolutionary patterns of our ancestors and the animal kingdom, including threat states like fight, flight and freeze. In the lives of our ancestors, let us not forget, the risks were very, very real: abandonment by the tribe or the family, exposure on the plains, predators in the jungle; these and many other risks could, and often would, lead to death. For almost the entirety of the existence of the human race that was the harsh reality and we have evolved to deal with a world where that is the case, where there is real, present danger.

In the world today, most of us are very rarely faced with a true life-or-death situation (and what a wonderful thing that is). Sometimes, though, our biology can leave us with a kind of short circuit: a faulty connection that we make subconsciously that causes an overload in what we feel in response to a situation. This happens because we are operating in a world that has changed beyond recognition compared to that of our ancestors. The instinctive parts of us, like the parts of our brains that are no different from those in lizards or other mammals, don't know everything our conscious mind knows, and they can act without our conscious thought. Sometimes those instinctive parts of us feel the significance of a situation without knowing, as our conscious mind does, that we are physically safe. They sense the importance of what is happening to us and act as though it literally means life or death, triggering physiological responses as if we were in genuine danger. These can be overwhelming or frightening to be inside, just like a faulty connection in an electric circuit can cause damage or start fires. In other words, when this short circuit happens, we move into our threat response: the defensive states of our nervous system described in Polyvagal Theory and elsewhere. In these situations, following curiosity toward this contraction, asking what is happening here and what you are frightened of, deep down, can often lead to awareness of deep evolutionary fears like abandonment or death. This kind of confusion from our instincts is why public speaking regularly tops surveys of people's biggest fears: our instinctive parts think that we are actually at risk of death from the judgment of an audience, even if our rational mind knows this isn't the case.

Once we see these deep, underlying fears for what they are, we can forgive ourselves the stresses we feel: if part of me believes my entire existence is at risk here, then no wonder I am incredibly anxious. With that greater perspective, we can acknowledge the fear for what it is and also see in the light of day that it is unfounded in the present. This leads (sometimes very quickly) to a lessening of the fear and contraction and enables us to see that *we can choose*.

After my break-up, emotional and evolutionary triggers were regularly happening in my life and so I experimented with

Guy's idea and focused my curiosity on the contractions. In my experiments, I found that the hypothesis held true. It wasn't always easy and it didn't always work right away, but overall, it made a difference. As I looked inward at what was happening for me when I felt a contraction, things shifted and some of the reaction eased. Often, this was about a shift from blaming myself to understanding myself. That understanding allowed me to integrate my behaviour, see that I had been doing my best and forgive myself. That, in turn, lessened the power of the contraction in the moment and, over time, allowed me to understand more about my Deeper Self, developing my resilience to contraction. I began to contract less and become more skilled at bouncing back when I did. More than that, I began to heal and to grow.

Choose Responsibility

There is another thread to draw out here, which also originates for me in that discussion between Ewan and Guy and which complements the idea that *curiosity is the antidote to contraction*. It takes us back to an idea I first introduced in Chapter One: that suffering is caused not by what is actually here now, but by resisting what is actually here now. Here in Chapter Three, what this means is that, fundamentally, it isn't possible for one person to trigger someone else. That is, if I am triggered, it is not because of the actions of the person who has said or done something. It is *my interpretation* of those words or actions that caused me to feel triggered, whether that interpretation happened near the surface or deep in my subconscious.

Choosing to believe this is vitally important because it puts us fully in control of our own experience. It was this idea, along with the new antidote I had to my contractions, that helped me feel the kind of 'better' that I wanted after my break-up. *I can choose* to believe that my emotional reaction is my responsibility and not something to be blamed on someone else, not something that just happens to me. When I believe this, it takes me out of the victim mindset and into control of my life. *I can choose.*

Does this mean that we shouldn't blame people for cruel things they say or do to other people? No, it doesn't. As individuals and as societies, we have to set boundaries for what is acceptable and unacceptable behaviour. Sometimes we have to hold people to account when they cross those boundaries, with our judgment at times like those enhanced by asking '*What if everyone is doing their best?*' However, even when someone has behaved unacceptably, it is almost always better for the victim of that behaviour to believe that they have the power to choose their response to it.

For some readers, this will feel like an enormous idea: that the feelings we have come from our interpretation of events, not from the events themselves. From when we are children, we tell each other things like 'you made me sad,' but as we grow, we may come to take this new perspective – 'I make me sad' – and see powerful results.

For me, wrapped in a cycle of triggers and contractions, this belief was transformational. If it's up to me, I can change it. I am not a victim of the situation: my response is down to my interpretation, so it is within my power to choose something different.

Unfortunately, there is another side to this coin. There is a freedom in being able to affect what happens inside us, but it is a kind of dreadful freedom, because suddenly, everything is down to us. If *you can choose* whether you are triggered or not, then that is a lot of responsibility to hold. It takes courage to choose that, instead of placing the blame outside yourself, but it is worth it. If you are committed to deepening your understanding of yourself and to spending more of your time as your Higher Self, this is the only adventure to choose. It is the adventure of a creator, not a victim; the adventure of contracting less and less in our lives; the adventure of growing more capable and more skilful as we navigate the complexities of life. It is the adventure of taking responsibility not just for our actions in the world, but for how we interpret the actions of others.

What if it isn't that person, that event, that is upsetting me? What if instead it is my interpretation of the person and event that is causing me to feel this way?

There lies our responsibility.

It's Not About the Suits

It's not always easy to take that responsibility. Even if you are committed to this journey, as I am, it can sometimes be very hard to choose curiosity in the moment and follow it to the understanding that helps.

When we were planning our wedding, my wife and I were sitting on our balcony, having a conversation about some of the logistics of the event. We had moved to the balcony because I was struggling, getting anxious and stressed. but it didn't get better out there; in fact, it got worse. I can feel it now, sitting there, faced with a 'simple' situation about ushers and suits. Who would be ushers and who in the wedding party would wear what? It somehow wasn't simple, though: I couldn't speak, I couldn't *think*. My normally incredibly active, rational mind was completely still. Worse than still: empty, scarily empty. I sat, looking at the balcony rail, unable to look at Emma. I was waiting desperately for a thought to come, grasping for it. Anything. I wanted to say something, to talk it through with her. Nothing came. No thoughts, no words.

It was frightening and it is clear that this wasn't about what Emma was saying or doing, and it wasn't about ushers or suits or any of the logistics. Instead, something was taking me to a historical experience: a different place, a different time.

I spoke about this with my psychotherapist and he suggested a way to work with it if it came up again. First, notice what's happening: 'Ah, I'm shutting down here. I'm getting triggered.' Then, he suggested, get curious: 'That thing is happening. What is going on?'[3]

He went further: "It might be hard to do that yourself sometimes. You could even ask Emma for help. She could say: 'It looks like you're shutting down, Robbie. What's happening?'"

A week later, after sharing this suggestion with Emma, we were having another conversation about the wedding and it was happening again. Emma caught it: I could see it was difficult for her – she was getting frustrated with our exchange – but she managed to catch it anyway, assumed I was doing my best and said, "Robbie, you're shutting down. What's going on?" She caught it quite early and, even then, it was still hard for me to shift out of the contraction. I struggled to bring curiosity in the face of that question, but managed get outside the contraction just enough.

After a minute or so, I found I could speak through it and I shared what was going on in that moment: 'If I can't even make this decision about suits, how can I support you when you need my help? And how can we work together for the rest of our lives?' Her curiosity, engaging mine and then enabling me to share what was really happening for me, did shift the contraction. The openness and access to my rational mind returned to me, a little in the moment and then more over subsequent minutes and hours, and I found myself gradually returning to my calm, adult self. Only from that place could I solve the problem and make the decisions.

Curiosity Is the Antidote to Contraction

Later, through more conversations and more curiosity about another deep contraction around the wedding and the suits, I saw two more stories at play, two memories from another time. My fears about our relationship were real and voicing them allowed me to shift into curiosity, but these memories were the historical events that were being triggered in me.

The first is a story of being trapped and alone without the answer, feeling cornered. Perhaps the story of a small boy, home educated by incredibly understanding parents and then later sent to a primary school with people who didn't understand him, a place with *so many* rules he didn't know and questions he couldn't answer. *Alone and without the answer, feeling trapped and afraid.*

The second is a story of just wanting everyone to be happy. Perhaps the story of a small boy in a family struggling with the challenges of step-children and long-distance relationships: a mother who wants her partner to move to live with her; a father who is struggling to juggle his son and partner in one town and another son from a previous relationship in a city many miles away, and a half-brother who, underneath it all, just wants his father to come home. And a small boy who *just wants everyone to be happy, together.*

And somehow, in awareness of those stories, everything becomes easier. Next time, I have more perspective on what is happening as I find myself alone and without the answer, feeling trapped and afraid, or as I find myself stuck, unable to make things work because I just want everyone to be happy, together, which isn't always possible. I know where those feelings, those contractions, come from; I can see them and I can forgive myself for finding them hard. If someone else had been through those things, well, they would probably find the same things hard, too.

So, these contractions shift from being simply what is, simply what happens to me, to being something I can see: a historical experience, a memory, a story I tell myself. Then, the next time I find myself contracting from that same historical experience, I am a little less trapped, unable to speak or move or decide, and a little less the time after that and the time after that and so on. They are parts of me: the young boy alone and without the answer and the even younger boy who just wants everyone to be happy, together. They deserve to be loved, not pushed away, just like all the other parts of me do.

I can use *curiosity is the antidote to contraction*. I can get outside of those stories, and then *I can choose*.

It's not about the suits, Robbie. It's about the last 40 years.

The Patterns That Keep Us Safe

This is just one example, but I could have shared many from my own life, as situations like this show up and I struggle. I could tell you client stories about the energy shift for people when they understand and then integrate into themselves the memory that has been triggered. This often happens, like it did for me, when they can see the time in their past from where the stories they tell themselves originated. They see that, at those times, it was perfectly understandable to feel and react as they did: it kept them safe. It really helped back then, but now, in the present day, they don't need that help in the same way. They can love the memory or part of themselves that is causing trouble instead of trying to shut it down and push it away.

Perhaps the contractions we feel once protected us. Perhaps sitting on the balcony unable to think or speak is the freeze mechanism from the part of my brain I share with other animals, but they don't help us anymore. Not really. Almost all the time in the modern day, this part of us is an outdated mechanism that doesn't make anything better for us, but can absolutely make things worse, like the rabbit in the headlights, freezing in vain as the car races towards it.

If you are triggered in your work, the way to succeed in work is not through contracting further. We don't do our best work when we are fighting, fleeing or freezing.

In your relationships, the great joy that love brings to you and your partner doesn't manifest when you are contracting, but it could be worse: your reactions from within a contraction will often carry pain and arguments and hurt to those you love, as a response from your own fear, which originated in another time.

With your children, the guidance and wisdom they need is hard to come by when your chest is tight and your fear is high.

If you are committed to living as your Higher Self, to being the person who you are on your best days more as your life goes on, then the idea that *curiosity is the antidote to contraction* is fundamental.

Guilt Is the Path to Growth

If you use *curiosity is the antidote to contraction*, you will learn more about yourself. As we learn and develop new perspectives on ourselves and our lives, our decision-making processes become more effective and sophisticated. Sometimes, looking back with more wisdom and perspective, we realise that things we did and choices we made in the past are not things we would do now. Once we have greater perspective on the deeper parts of ourselves, we may see behaviour in a new light and, upon reflection, we may find new regret for the ways we have behaved. This brings us back to guilt and shame, as I described them in Chapter Two.

Guilt is healthy. It is realising we have done something in the past (sometimes the very recent past) that contradicts how we now think people should behave, that contradicts how we would be as our Higher Selves. Guilt is *I did something bad*. It is *I did something I'd rather not do again*. Guilt is how we learn. It shows us we have developed our perspective and our ability to respond skilfully to the challenges of the world because we know something different from what we knew then. It is how we decide 'never again' and 'it will be different next time.' It is how our wisdom, skill and nobility grow.

Shame is a different beast altogether. Shame is being unable to distinguish one's actions from oneself. Shame, remember, is *I am bad*.

Guilt, on the one hand, helps us to be socialised creatures and to gradually adjust our behaviour towards the skilful, wise, noble person we are on our best days. Shame, on the other hand, teaches us that there are parts of ourselves that *shouldn't be*. It wraps us in patterns that stop us owning, accepting and integrating parts of ourselves.

To use all our strengths fully, to make an impact in the world and be our Higher Selves, we need *all* parts of us to be at our disposal. Only with all parts of us at our disposal can we truly fulfil our potential, can we truly be our most skilful and wise. And so, if we are truly committed to using our strengths, to making the biggest contribution we can, we need to develop perspective on our shame and reintegrate those parts of ourselves that we have pushed away.

The Castle

Writer and coach, Vegard Olsen, talks about this using the image of a castle. When we are young, we run around the castle, playing freely in any part of it with the beautiful freedom of a child. As our life goes on, we learn that certain parts of the castle are not safe for children and maybe not safe for anyone. We might learn that 'good little children' don't go there. We learn this from our parents, from our teachers, from our siblings and from our internal interpretations of what we see in the world around us.

The top of a tower, perhaps, or a dark room in a cellar, is unsafe or is where 'good boys' or 'good girls' don't go, so we don't go there, but we are children when we hear these messages and sometimes we confuse them. We are so frightened of what might happen at the *top* of the tower or in that *particular* room in the cellar that we don't go in the tower or cellar at all. Out of fear of accessing that one particular room, we deny ourselves access to a whole part of the castle, a whole part of our playground, a whole part of our selves.

For me, at the top of one of my towers is the kind of anger that could lead to physical harm to someone. Only bad people get angry like that, I tell myself. Perhaps I *am* bad when I am angry like that, so I will not go there again. But somewhere I got confused: I haven't locked just the top floor; I've locked the whole tower. Somewhere lower down that same tower are other, smaller, less dangerous parts of that same emotion, anger: the ability to stand up for myself or others, the ability to be direct with people, the ability to speak my mind when it might offend someone. The ability to debate healthily with someone else is there, too, as is the ability to express my frustration when someone oversteps my boundaries. These things are perfectly healthy, acceptable things for any adult to do in the course of their daily life. More than that, without them I am powerless in certain situations: life happens to me and I can't find the ability to respond. I deeply admire people who can be direct, people who are able to debate with others with clarity and humour, people who express their frustration rather than letting it fester. My Higher Self is someone who can do all these things, I *know* it is, but with the tower locked, my ability to do each of these things is locked away, too. My ability to be myself is reduced. My ability to create change for myself, my loved ones and the world is lessened.

The key distinction, again, is between guilt and shame.

Shame is *I am bad* if I go into this tower, if I access any of those things. Shame is a fixed way of being and requires a fixed response: a lock on the door of the tower, which hides and restricts certain parts of ourselves, at all costs and in all situations.

Guilt is knowing that *acting in a certain way* is bad. Guilt gives you the power to choose: will I do it again this time or will I be different? How much of this quality should I use in this moment? Guilt is the tower left open, unlocked, so *I can choose*. With guilt (healthy, important guilt), I know what could happen if I go to the top floor of the tower at the wrong time or in the wrong way. I know it may be unsafe. I know it may conflict with my values and how I want to be. The top of the tower is there and available to me and I *choose* not to go there. I don't need to lock it away and, at the same time, lock away the other floors of the tower. Instead, I can integrate and own the things I have done and the person I am, regretting, forgiving and knowing I will do better next time. This is what we need to be able to do if we are to access our potential.

Without guilt, some of our potential to grow and change for the better is lost.

The stories I have told in this chapter started very much from a realisation that I had not been the person I wanted to be in my previous relationship. I had made mistakes and I had hurt someone about whom I cared deeply. I hadn't done anything terrible, by most measures, but there were many ways I could have been better in the relationship. One of the important ways I was supported in the aftermath of that break-up was to stay in guilt and not shame. I remember now the words of my mother on several different occasions, giving me the message: yes, you could have done better, but you are not a bad person. What a powerful message to give to our children, young and fully grown.

Curiosity Is the Antidote to Contraction

That wasn't the first time that I have behaved as I would rather not have done and I'm sure it won't be the last. In each of my romantic relationships, there are things I wish I hadn't done. I have said things I really wish I hadn't said. I have let down, even betrayed, friends. I have been violent, although thankfully not since schoolyard fights. I think about many of these things regularly. They come into my mind with at least a wince and sometimes a much stronger physical reaction. A contraction. As I engage my curiosity on that contraction, what I realise is that the contraction is a message: *I don't want to behave like that again. I don't want to forget these events: I want to remember them, to savour them to make sure that next time I choose to do something different.*

I don't always manage to live up to my values, but through guilt and curiosity, my mistakes become the foundations and building blocks of the person I am and the person I want to be in the future.

Follow the contraction of your guilt and get curious. You will see what you want to change about yourself, what value you did not live up to, what you want to be different next time. Seeing those things gives us a choice, a freedom, to make next time better. When we face these things, we can say to ourselves, 'OK, maybe I didn't live up to the standards I set myself or those others set for me, but what if I was doing my best?' This way, you can maintain access to your potential by leaving the tower in the castle open but choosing not to go there, rather than locking it away in shame.

Your curiosity about all this, bit by bit, day by day, is vital to helping you grow. It might take time and commitment with some of the things you regret, especially if the regret runs deep, but engage the curiosity: go back to those questions from Chapter Two, but turn them on yourself now. What did it take for me to behave like that? What is going on here?

You might need some help. It's a scary and sometimes painful adventure to understand our shame, to forgive ourselves, to move to guilt and then closer and closer still to the Higher Self. It's scary, but it's worth it.

How Do I Do This?

This chapter is about how to use curiosity to dance the dance with the unconscious parts of your Deeper Self. It is about using curiosity to grow in your capacities and capabilities for dealing with the complexity of the modern world, by looking at the tangles of your psychology.

As we face people or things that are 'triggering us'[4] and get curious, we will find out what it is that leaves us feeling contracted. We will uncover memories and patterns from our past, stories that may be forming a fundamental part of how we relate to ourselves or to others. Curiosity will give us the perspective to see these memories and patterns more as they actually are. Once we realise that our behaviour, our patterns and the ways we are acting are sometimes a part of our past, part memory and part stories we tell ourselves, we realise that we have a choice. Looking at the patterns and responses that carry us into these contractions gives us the perspective we need so that *we can choose*.

Once I learned that *curiosity is the antidote to contraction*, I embraced curiosity by delving into myself, into my experience, my history and my assumptions.

A new habit began to form. The contraction – a feeling impossible to ignore – was now followed by curiosity. The questions were: 'What's *really* happening here? I'm not at risk of death, even if it feels like that. I'm not even at risk of harm. So, what is *actually*

Curiosity Is the Antidote to Contraction

going on?' I began to *feel* the power of the key idea of this chapter. By shining the light of curiosity on myself, using the understanding I had picked up through books, podcasts and conversations, I found myself, in the end, opening up. I felt more of my contractions dissipate under the light of curiosity like mist in the morning sun. More than that: each contraction became an opportunity, a chance to learn even more about my Deeper Self, a chance to free myself from another chain that might keep me from the man I really wanted to be: my Higher Self.

When I was younger, I used to have a kind of vocal tick, a way to slow the conversation down to give myself time to think or to avoid getting things wrong. I used to say, 'Mmm…interesting.' Now, that has become a part of the way I shift from contraction to curiosity.

When something unexpected happens, particularly when your emotions crack like a whip and your tensions or your tears rise, you can deny and you can fight. You can even strive, desperately, for openness, but those options won't take you out of contraction or the sense of being trapped; they won't give you a sense of possibility or greater access to your Higher Self. What you need is curiosity. In times like that, '*Mmm…interesting*' can be your tool. Use it to shift.

Bring humour and a smile with it, if you can: 'Mmm… interesting! Wow, what is happening here? What part of my hilarious and wonderful and flawed humanity may have got confused and befuddled here? What am I up to? What's going on, *really?*'

Bring love with it: 'Mmm…interesting. There's something deep happening here, something from the past. No wonder I'm struggling with it. I am human, after all. What could *really* be going on?'

It isn't always easy to stop the contractions and make that shift. Sometimes you'll need help from someone around you, noticing when you find yourself trapped in contraction, as Emma helped me with the suits.

If we want to help someone else, we might use language like my psychotherapist suggested to me. We might use the language that psychologist, Peter Levine, suggests: "Gosh it seems like you're feeling upset. I'm just wondering how you experience that right now and I'd be really glad to be here with you when you experience that."[5]

One of the significant contributions of both Levine's work and Polyvagal Theory more broadly is to connect our bodily experience to our psychology. The impact of this connection works both ways. Our psychological response can affect the state of our physical nervous system (causing it to contract), but also by changing our physical state, we can affect our psychology. In the times when we find shifting to curiosity particularly difficult, this can be important and that is why Levine suggests becoming open and curious to the *sensations* we feel in our body and allowing that curiosity to help us to shift our states.

"If we can become even a little bit open and curious to these sensations, they will change," says Levine.

Author and consultant, Jamie Wheal, suggests a way to 'hack' our biology in times we feel under threat or feel we may be moving that way. He recommends what is called vagal tone breathing. Breathe out over a count of 10, hold your breath out for two seconds and then fill your lungs. Repeating this five times can be all we need to shift out of defensive states, especially if we add in keeping our eyes open but with a soft focus and breathing out with a hum[6]. This, in turn, makes curiosity more easily available.

When you can engage your curiosity, follow it. Let it lead you towards remembering and understanding some part of yourself better. Allow your curiosity to lead you towards owning that part of you and integrating it into your view of the world, accepting it as part of your Deeper Self. With that new perspective, you can find more agency to act differently, to choose to act as your Higher Self, and also to change yourself, at that deepest and most fundamental level. You can begin to think 'Do I want to act from this set of beliefs or memories? Or do I want to choose a different belief here?'

Not all of the things we are dealing with involve delving into deep feelings from our past, into those childhood patterns and stories, but sometimes the changes we seek in ourselves do require looking in deep places. The path away from contraction and towards possibility is a strange one: it involves a counterintuitive facing of the things that are difficult to face. It takes courage. Through examination of these deep places, we increase our understanding and, as we learn about them and ourselves, they become easier to face. As we accept the things we have done as understandable actions, we can regret them while still knowing *I was doing the best I could with what I had at the time*. At this point, they become easier to hold and to own and then we become easier to love.

This process is hardest when we are in deep pain, when we are filled with regret, when we think 'I am a terrible person,' 'I am a broken person,' and it starts with a small step. Perhaps now is the time to change your thinking, to choose a different adventure. It isn't about shame; you are not a bad person. It is about guilt and the path from shame to guilt and on to possibility and it starts with asking yourself a question. It starts with getting curious.

CHAPTER THREE SUMMARY

Key idea: When you feel yourself contracting, becoming more upset, anxious or reactive, use the key idea of this chapter: *curiosity is the antidote to contraction*. When we use our curiosity to face our struggles, we can shift out of our defensive states and develop a greater understanding of our Deeper Selves. With this, we can choose to step away from our instinctive patterns and reactions and towards our Higher Selves.

Exercises, practices and questions for reflection:

- **What if this person/event isn't *actually* upsetting me?** What if instead my interpretation of the person/event is what is causing me to feel this way?

- **Remember: It's not about the chicken and it's not about the suits.** When you feel a trigger and a contraction, it is almost never about what is happening in the moment. Instead, it is taking you back to something deeper. Try to bring curiosity in the moment: what is *really* happening here? And, in the moment or later, look for any links to memories: when do you first remember feeling a feeling like that? Who does it remind you of?

- **Look for the ancient short circuits** when a fault (or confusion) in our internal 'wiring' may be leading to an overload to our system. When you find yourself afraid of something and you have a sense it may be not be completely rational, ask yourself: what am I frightened of, deep down? When you have an answer, try digging deeper: if that happens, *then* what am I frightened of, deep down?

See what emerges: if you see that your instincts are short-circuiting to an existential fear when none is present in reality (i.e. you aren't going to die in real life), you may be able to have more compassion for yourself about feeling such a strong response.

- Use **The Castle Metaphor.** Think of a person you really dislike. It could be someone you know or a famous person. Answer the question: what three qualities do you really dislike in this person? These may be qualities that you dislike so much that you have unknowingly closed off a whole tower of your castle to protect yourself from them. The game then is: what is a more acceptable, smaller version of each of those qualities? In my example from this chapter, I disliked and shut away anger, but that led to me also locking away other qualities like standing up for myself or others, being direct, speaking my mind when it might offend someone, debating healthily with someone else and expressing my frustration when someone oversteps my boundaries. What might be possible if you allowed yourself just 5% more access to the qualities you dislike in your daily life? What might that look like?

- **What's *really* happening here?** I'm not at risk of death, even if it feels like that; I'm not even at risk of harm. What is *actually* going on?

- **What if I was doing my best?** Maybe I didn't live up to the standards I set or those others set for me, but what if I was doing my best? Yes, I could have behaved better, but I am not a bad person; I am doing my best.

- **What did it take for me to behave like that?** What is going on here? Where is this feeling of guilt or shame coming from?

- **'Mmm…interesting.'** Develop a habit of bringing this phrase to mind when you notice the contractions. Bring humour and a smile with it, if you can: 'Mmm…interesting! Wow, what is happening here? What part of my hilarious and wonderful and flawed humanity is confused or befuddled here? What am I up to? What's going on, *really*?' Or bring love with it: 'Mmm…interesting. There's something deep happening here, something from the past. No wonder I'm struggling with it. What could *really* be going on?'

- **Bring curiosity to your bodily experience.** Become curious, if you can, about the physical sensations of a contraction or help someone else do the same. If that is too difficult, remember vagal tone breathing: breathe out over a count of 10, hold out for two and then fill your lungs.

Further Reading and Learning

- Guy Sengstock: guysengstock.com

- Ewan Townhead: www.ewantownhead.com

- *The Science and Psychology of Polarisation* by Rebel Wisdom, featuring interviews with Steven Porges, Peter Levine and Jamie Wheal among others:
  www.youtube.com/watch?v=EUNHj5eh7BM

- *Pathways to Possibility* by Rosamund Stone Zander

PART TWO

CHAPTER FOUR

NO ONE CAN COMPETE WITH YOU AT BEING YOU

Part One contains the three key ideas of this book, outlined to support you to live more as your Higher Self, with all the potential benefits outlined in the introduction. They have done this for me and I will continue to use them. But reading a book doesn't change our lives by itself. You have to apply the ideas; you have to practise.

Part Two provides further stories, practices and inspiration to help you to apply the ideas from Part One. I will focus on two areas that often provide the biggest challenges to living as our Higher Selves whilst simultaneously being fundamental parts of how most people think of a life well-lived: our work (in this chapter) and our romantic relationships (in Chapter Five). The topics we'll cover are ones where I and people I have worked with have found ourselves most often contracting, most often stressed, most often lost in the confusion of complexity, most often needing to use the ideas from Part One. They warrant closer examination because of their potential to hold us back or trap us where we are. They are areas where our ways of seeing the world may require upgrading to ones fitter for the complexity of the world in which we live.

As we discussed in the introduction, to make a contribution in the face of the increasingly complex challenges facing the human race, each of us must find the place in the world where we can bring our unique mix of skills and experiences to bear. Each year, most of us spend hundreds or thousands of hours working, so if we want to use our unique strengths to make the biggest contribution we can, we will often want to do that through our work. Our Higher Selves and our values often call on us to make an impact that is meaningful to us, but this isn't easy. The patterns and pitfalls of our Deeper Selves can hold us back or tie us in knots around our work, especially when it matters most to us. This chapter will, I hope, support you to take the steps towards work that is more fulfilling and that enables you to make your meaningful contribution to the world.

At the very least, it is here to make the difficult moments of that journey a little easier. At best, the ideas in this chapter and this book can help you simultaneously make a greater contribution and learn about yourself in the ways that matter most, making yourself more skilful now and for the future.

There are many ways in which the ideas in this book can be applied to our workplaces and we have already seen some of them in Part One. However, throughout my work with clients who are wrestling with how to make their contribution, there is one area in particular that has reared its head again and again: the way we find ourselves locked in feelings of competition and comparison with others. This is not only a common obstacle, but also often one of the most damaging and challenging to overcome: causing stress, holding us back from making an impact and much more[1]. Choosing differently around competition has given me (and many people I have shared these ideas with) more freedom and agency to act in the world: shifting out of a feeling of being stuck and releasing our Higher Selves in a way that enables greater contribution and greater enjoyment throughout the challenges of a career.

Moving people through these traps of competition and comparison and into contribution is a vital part of unlocking the creative potential of the population. As we'll see, it also requires each of us to take greater perspective on ourselves, upgrading the way we see the world to create more complexity fitness.

The Comparison Age

There's a reason competition shows up as a struggle for so many of us: the Internet has given us an unparalleled ability to compare ourselves to others. When I was at school in the pre-social media days, things were different. It wasn't too hard to find a way in which I was actually winning at some competition among my peers. And the same was true for most people, both children and adults. Back then, you just had to be among the best greengrocers or artists or lawyers in the local area. In the present day, there is always someone, somewhere, who you can see is doing your job more successfully than you (and often there are *many* people you can see doing that). It can be exhausting. These competitions are occasionally real – we are competing for the same contract or client or job – but are mostly imagined or irrelevant to our actual work. They existed before the Internet, but were invisible to us and so had no impact on our lives. The online world has made comparisons with those around us an almost unavoidable part of modern life.

Over the following pages, I will tell a story of when I came face-to-face with this sense of competition. In this case, I didn't even need the Internet to find this person; he just showed up one weekend. I will use this story to draw out how a particular mix of fears and assumptions can catch us out and hold us back. It is about our careers and our work, but it is also about how that combination of fears and assumptions can hold us back anywhere in our lives. I have seen this show up so many times with my coaching clients.

A false sense of competition can hold us back from owning who we are and following that to the next level of our success. It's important to know this and to see it for what it is so that each of us realises that *we can choose*.

The Barbecue

I trained as a coach with The Coaching School, a training start-up based in London. When I joined, a big part of the school's appeal to me was its small scale: small cohorts, a tight-knit community of coaches who had been carefully selected and were put through truly excellent training. An unexpected bonus I can see now was that at first, during the training, there weren't many people there who I could compare myself directly with, except people in my cohort and others who had been coaching for much longer than I had, like our teachers.

The Coaching School worked hard to bring together its current students and alumni, providing space for people to meet, for ideas to mingle and for new friendships and partnerships to emerge. At one such gathering – a summer barbecue, about a year after starting my coaching business – I spoke to a coach who was taking The Coaching School's course the year after me. We did the normal 'getting to know you' conversation, but as it carried on and he talked about how well his fledgling coaching practice was going, the smile on my face became increasingly fixed. The feeling of warmth and encouragement inside me drained away and something very different emerged: anxiety rising, panic building, tension in my chest. It was the kind of contraction I spoke about in detail in Chapter Three. I am a reasonably competent actor, so I imagine my smile continued to appear mostly natural, even as deep inside I was becoming more and more pained.

This wasn't the first time I had felt this when confronted by someone with whom fears about comparison were triggered in me, as I will explain. I have had this feeling with everyone from people I've never met to close friends. Spending time on social media is a hotbed of these experiences for me. Thanks to the ideas in this book, while I still get these feelings, I have them less often and I can dance with them far more effectively.

Back at the barbecue, there I was with another coach – someone younger and less experienced than me – nonchalantly sharing his success. I can't know how this came across to other people there, but the contraction I felt affected the rest of the barbecue for me. Not only that, but it spread out into the rest of my week and then into the week after that. It was paralysing: it stopped me creating, it stopped me working effectively on my business, it made it harder to be present with clients and it made me unhappy. My coach at the time, Joel Monk, provided invaluable support with this, helping me to use *curiosity is the antidote to contraction*. Joel observed that the state I found myself in after the conversation was a place of scarcity and competition. With his help, as I turned my curiosity on the situation, I turned up three key elements that seemed to be playing a part in my reaction.

To Care Deeply Is to Be Vulnerable

The first was that I really cared about what I was doing. I still do. As with most or perhaps all contractions, this one was about fear and a part of that fear was present because of how much I cared.

There is a difficult truth, which is that if we let something matter to us deeply, we become vulnerable, and vulnerability contains risk. Having something that matters to us in our lives has the potential to reward us with fulfilment and meaning. It also leaves us vulnerable to that thing being taken away. I've spoken to clients who said things like 'I don't want to look too closely at whether I should leave this company because I know what I'll find.' For them, it felt safer to stay in ignorance. It was too much for them to step away from 'safe and stable' to take risks for something they might love. To care deeply about something is an act of courage, acting in the face of fear that we might lose or, indeed, fail to find something we care about. In the long term, though, a life without anything or anyone we care deeply about is no life. That's why, in the end, avoidant sentiments like 'I don't want to look too closely because I know what I'll find' are unsustainable.

If you feel a deep contraction in a situation of comparison or competition, then using your curiosity can help you learn more about what really matters to you. It might be a person; it might be your fledgling coaching business; it might be something deeper. Understanding this allows us to be more compassionate when we find ourselves contracting: 'It makes sense that I am worried about this; it's something I really care about.'

Using *curiosity is the antidote to contraction* also allows us to deepen our understanding of what scares us. When our fear taps into the challenges of a human evolved for simpler times facing the complexity of today, that can make things even more difficult.

By the time I went to the barbecue, I already knew what was at the root of most of my fears about failing in my business. I had learnt this starkly and powerfully when an early client agreed to work with me and then changed her mind. I remember sitting on the sofa going hot and cold, tears stinging my eyes, feeling humiliated and unable to speak, because a woman changed her mind and didn't want to pay me £300. Of course, it's not about the woman changing her mind, Robbie, and it's not about the £300. It's about millennia of evolution. With the help of my coach, I dug in, using a nested set of questions about fear to get to an increasing level of understanding about what was happening in my Deeper Self.

'If this woman says no to you, what are you afraid of?'
'That I don't have enough clients.'
Then the next question: 'If you don't have enough clients, what are you afraid of?'
'That this business won't work.'
'If this business doesn't work, what are you afraid of?'
'I'll have to tell everyone I've failed.'
'If you have to tell everyone you've failed, what are you afraid of?'
I felt frustrated because it felt stupid to say it, but the answer that came was: 'I'll be abandoned.'

In our evolutionary past, as we've discussed and will come back to, abandonment meant death. This is the kind of evolutionary short circuit I mentioned in Chapter Three and this is often what we discover if we dig into the social fears we have: whilst our life is not at risk, something in the way we are experiencing the world overloads our system with a disproportionate amount of fear because it 'thinks' that our very existence is at stake. That, at least, makes it more understandable why I may be so triggered by a woman changing her mind or a man at a barbecue.

This is what I mean when I talk about the value of understanding our Deeper Selves: knowing the things that matter to us at this level allows us, at the times when something triggers us, to see what is happening. Once we can see what is happening, we can take perspective and choose to respond as our Higher Selves.

How Can I Compete with *That*?

As I felt the contraction begin at the barbecue, the coach was telling me about his background as a director at a training company that works with big businesses. And I mean big ones: ones we have all heard of, including a role with one of the most famous brands in the world. When I asked about the work specifically, he used the term 'C-suite.' This kind of term often triggered feelings of inadequacy in me at the time, with opaque jargon regularly leaving me in contraction[2]. Luckily, by this point, at least I knew what it meant[3], but even knowing the term, the conversation was exposing something that felt real and important: the gap between my network and his. He had a network that included really senior people in really big companies, people who could and probably did pay *a lot* for coaching. Not only that, but the coach had more clients than I'd had at the equivalent point in my training. Even more, if I remember correctly, than I did a year later as I was talking to him! He was younger than me, too, and hadn't been coaching as long.

As I turned my curiosity on myself (with the help of my coach), the second element in the situation gradually emerged. Catching the thoughts in the previous paragraph, I was able to notice just how many assumptions I was making.

I was asking questions like, 'What chance do I have of making a living out of coaching when someone else is younger, has done less training and yet has more clients than I do, as well as a network of incredibly rich, successful people who trust him? How can I compete with *that*?'

Gradually, I was able to take perspective on those thoughts. Questions began to come up: 'Hang on, what does his age have to do with me making a living out of coaching?' 'Why should the relative amount of training we have done count for so much?' 'What does his network have to do with my ability to grow a business?'

Before I looked at those questions slowly and carefully, I had been making assumptions: that being older should mean having a better network; that more training should bring some divine right to more success; that if my network looks worse, then it is worse and there's nothing I can do about it. From this, I made deeper assumptions. If all this is true, then I can't possibly compete with this person. Perhaps most damagingly: if I can't compete with this person, then I might as well give up. Remember the nine dots puzzle from Chapter One and you will see that I had invented a set of rules that were making this a game I couldn't win.

When I slowed right down and focused my curiosity, the underlying rule I was creating was something like this:

If this person is succeeding, then I can't succeed, because my success in my business is dependent on competing with and beating them.

We can see how this might have been a natural and useful assumption in simpler times. Way back in our evolution, or even a few decades ago, my success might have been dependent on the failure of someone else in the area. Maybe there really is only space for one greengrocer in the village. However, in a 21st century city or a career that can be delivered online, the assumption is clearly flawed.

It is the equivalent of adding 'without using the space outside the dots' in the nine dots puzzle and I believe it is, along with its many close relations, a scourge of our times. It holds people back from truly engaging with their strengths in the world and it traps many of us in exhausting competitions that we can never win. Seeing it for what it is – invented and false – frees us to choose something very different.

These false assumptions about competition, which stopped me solving the puzzle of my life, were the second element of what was happening for me at the barbecue.

Perhaps at the barbecue there were other ways I could have got myself out of this contraction. I could have consoled myself by pretending the other coach was lying. I could have imagined he was failing miserably in other parts of his life, perhaps his relationships, and that his coaching success was irrelevant as a result. I could have pretended that I didn't want to work with the kind of people who were in his network anyway. Those things might well have given me a little relief or let me off the hook, but they are all forms of denial taking me further from an understanding of the truth by layering assumption on assumption on assumption. That might feel good in the moment, but it doesn't serve in the long term. By this point, I was already committed to the journey of this book, wherever it would take me: the journey of gaining more and more perspective so that *I can choose*, the journey to living more as my Higher Self. For that journey, I needed the truth.

To help me find the truth, I used (not without discomfort) *curiosity is the antidote to contraction*. I also used *what if everyone is doing their best?* I remembered Brené Brown's husband Steve (see Chapter Two) and his sense that, by taking that idea to heart, he could see more clearly what actually is rather than focusing on what could or should be. What if the coach at the barbecue wasn't lying and he wasn't a failure elsewhere? What if he was doing his best and was a Grade A coach? If all those things were true, then what?

Those questions took me out of the need to come up with new assumptions that papered over cracks and instead helped me to strip away assumptions and see what actually was. What actually was, at least in that moment, was one of the most important questions I have discovered on the journey of living as my Higher Self and taking my strengths out into the world. That is: *why do I need to compete with this person anyway?*

This question is the new rule we need to replace the falseness of our 'without using the space outside the dots' assumption about competition. It reminds us that our assumptions of competition are often not as real as they seem.

When Fear and Competition Collide

Let's bring this together.

First, when we care deeply about something, we become vulnerable, which brings with it the fear that we might lose or fail at something we care about. Second, our unconscious mind often bases our responses to the world on a set of false assumptions about competition. When these things combine, it's almost always tough, but when it gets really damaging for our day-to-day lives is when the fear that is triggered in us is a deep, evolutionary fear, a part of our Deeper Selves that can short-circuit and feel life-threatening. This is the third element of what was happening to me at the barbecue: the kind of super-contraction that happens to many of us across our lives when a deep evolutionary fear of abandonment or social exclusion combines with false assumptions. We slip into threat mode, which has a significant and residual effect, altering the quality of our lives and often holding us back significantly from acting in the real world.

This happened for me at the barbecue and, as I've already described, the results weren't good. The underlying fear was the one I had discovered was often found at the bottom of my contractions: that deep down I would have to give up on my work; that giving up would lead to humiliation and that, in some way, the humiliation would lead to abandonment and death.

If you discover something like this in yourself, you may end up, as I did, frustrated by the impossibly out-of-proportion feel of it, and so it is worth getting really clear about why our minds might short-circuit around these kinds of social fears, seeming to overwhelm us with an out-of-proportion response. Greater understanding gives us more opportunity to step out of the response and choose a different path.

Millennia ago, humiliation and the subsequent abandonment by our tribe really could lead to death. Stories about hunter-gatherer societies often sound beautiful to me – time in nature, tight-knit communities and more equality – but they can also contain the kind of utilitarian callousness that warrants the kind of fear we sometimes feel in social situations[4].

The Aché, a hunter-gatherer society that lived in the jungles of Paraguay until the 1960s and which Yuval Noah Harari describes in his book, *Sapiens*, viewed killing children, sick people and the elderly as a normal part of life. One of the reasons for this is that the Aché were hunted mercilessly by Paraguayan farmers and being mobile was incredibly important to them. Being slowed down by a sick child or an old man may have been the difference between the tribe surviving or not and this may have led to what appears to us as an incredibly harsh attitude. You can imagine how this need to be mobile may have been present for our hunter-gatherer ancestors, too. In evolutionary terms, then, the example of the Aché could demonstrate how it really can be a matter of life and death to stop being an asset to your tribe and become useless.

If being useless could be fatal to our ancestors, it would be evolutionarily useful to have a deep fear of your tribe finding out just how useless you are. Being the kind of useless person who can't even sell coaching to a woman who says she wants it, even for just a few hundred pounds, for instance. And what if there's already someone else in the tribe who does what you do, perhaps coaching and making money from it, but has a better network than you and is already doing it better than you do but with less experience? Why would the tribe want you in that case?

Both the fear we feel, then, and the contractions around competition can be deep, beyond even our childhood experiences. It can be an evolutionary pattern to help us to survive, originating millennia ago in the lives of our ancestors. It isn't an exaggeration to conclude that these moments when assumptions of competition are at play can feel deadly.

What is often required in these situations is firstly the taking of perspective: using *curiosity is the antidote to contraction* to understand more of what is happening. Then, it's courage: once we take steps forward to do the thing we are afraid of, we find clear, indisputable evidence that the fear of death wasn't real. We are still alive. Each time we take the steps, we gain confidence and, over time, we can find that the power of these contractions diminishes. To do that, though, we need to get moving and the combination of fears and assumptions can make that feel impossible.

Any pursuit of a calling, any attempt to make a real difference in the world, will give you plenty of opportunities to dance with these contractions. If we care deeply about our work, this leaves us vulnerable, and vulnerability always requires courage because it always includes fear. When we make our pursuit of a calling public, we also open ourselves to those deeper evolutionary fears of abandonment. If we believe in the power that comes from understanding our Deeper Selves, though, each and every one of these contractions gives us an opportunity to learn and grow. With curiosity, we delve deeper into ourselves, finding something that we hadn't seen before and giving ourselves more access to our Higher Selves.

However, these assumptions around competition can be insidious. In fact, they almost got the better of me long before the barbecue. Before, in fact, I had even started my coaching business.

As I worked to change career, in the end arriving in coaching, I felt plenty of fear because my career really mattered to me. I was scared every possibility might be another career dead-end that wasted more of my time. I was afraid of telling people that I wanted to change career because it made me vulnerable. I was scared that people would judge me in all kinds of ways when I told them about the different careers that interested me. And more.

I also had assumptions about competition because my brother was working as a coach at the time. I couldn't possibly compete with my brother, who already worked in coaching, with his extensive experience, amazing networks, fantastic writing and visionary projects. This brings us back to what we might call the key false assumption in this chapter: that for one person to succeed, someone else has to fail; that it's not possible for everyone to win.

In whatever part of your life you catch an assumption of competition, it's time to engage curiosity. In particular, ask these questions: what is actually true here? Do I actually need to compete with this person? Is my success actually dependent on their failure?

Occasionally, if you answer these questions, you may find times when your success actually is dependent on someone else's failure. For instance, when I started dating my wife, it helped me to know that she had recently been on dates with two other men, both of whom were interested in seeing her again. I actually was in competition.

Knowledge of a real competition can change the quality of the attention we give, our focus on timescales and many other things, which are less important if competition isn't present. If a client wants a proposal from you and you know they are receiving a proposal from three similar companies, that's really different to being in a long conversation with a client where they are going to work with you again and the two of you are just working out how.

Most of the time, the feeling of competition we have is simply an ancient instinct playing tricks on us in a modern, complex world. The competition isn't real at all.

Even in those times when your success actually does depend on someone else's failure, like when competing with other applicants for a job, we need to be careful how we relate to competition. It can be a trap that leads to inaction or withdrawal. By using *curiosity is the antidote to contraction*, we can take perspective on the competition in the cold light of day, release ourselves from the power of it and be freer to be at our best, to act as our Higher Selves. Given we are more skilful, wise and noble as our Higher Selves, success almost always becomes more likely. This was certainly true as I began to date my wife: the more I could be my relaxed, present, Higher Self, the better it seemed to go…and I came out victorious! If I had got too lost in the sense of competition, I might have simply given up on my fledgling relationship with Emma (this is not too farfetched an idea, particularly given the size of a bouquet that arrived for her in the early days…not from me).

Not only are our evolutionary instincts likely short-circuiting when it comes to fear of abandonment, but they are likely also at play with the sense of scarcity we have around competition: that one of us has to lose for the other to win. Back in the jungle or on the tundra with our tribe (or even further back, as a herd of animals somewhere, before human consciousness), the need to compete was far more real. We lived in much greater scarcity. There's only so much of a dead elk to go round. The one who gets to the elk last, or can't outcompete others for it, goes hungry. In the end, they might die. Perhaps it is this ancient wiring that leads us to assume scarcity where none exists.

You can see this in the assumption I was making that my success in building my business was dependent on competing with and beating the other coach. I assumed a scarcity of clients to coach and a scarcity of money to be made from coaching.

One way of looking at my career change into coaching is that I held back from it for at least a year and maybe longer because of how these unconscious assumptions of scarcity played out with my brother. The damaging assumption here was something like: if coaching is a calling for someone else in my family, then it can't be mine, too.

If you ask, 'What is actually true here?' then this clearly doesn't make any sense. Given that genes and upbringings often give similar strengths (and weaknesses) to siblings, it is almost certainly more likely that I might share a calling with my brother than that I would share a calling with a random stranger. That didn't stop my fears and assumptions about competition holding me back and it almost prevented me from pursuing a profession that, more than anything I have done before, allows me to use my strengths and make a contribution to the world.

The Purpose of Competition

It can be tempting in the face of all this to dismiss competition as an altogether bad and unhelpful thing, but remember part of the purpose of this book is to help all of us develop ways of looking at the world that deal better with its complexity. When we are doing this, we need to beware of black-and-white thinking like 'competition is bad' or 'competition is good.' Instead, we need to include both ends of a spectrum and live with a more nuanced, shades-of-grey idea like 'competition can *sometimes* be useful. Is this one of those times?'

Could competition here be fun and exciting, like the closing part of a close race for a championship in sport? Could it spur us on to important discoveries, as it can in science? Or to ever greater creativity, as it did with John Lennon and Paul McCartney? Or extraordinary goal-scoring feats as with Lionel Messi and Cristiano Ronaldo? Could it create extraordinary competence, skill and longevity as with Chris Evert and Martina Navratilova? Could competition drive prices down, making more services available more cheaply to more people? Could it force innovation, making businesses or organisations come up with new, novel ways to serve people or make a difference in the world?

Conversely, could it force us to cut corners leading to problems or disasters?[5] Could it encourage cheating and bad acting, like the drug use in cycling and athletics?

Crucially, for us, could it inspire us? Or could it wrap us up in scarcity and stop us from acting?

Our attitudes to competition in each and every case, then, are important. And they are something *we can choose*.

Ask yourself: is competition serving me here?

If you want to lose weight or push yourself in your business or create a new habit, having someone to compete with and measure your progress against can be really useful in keeping you on track. Apps like Strava help people facilitate friendly competitions with other runners and cyclists – and even compete with themselves – driving users to personal records.

It's not always useful, though. It isn't serving us when it leads to people holding back or giving up something they could do well because they believe they can't compete. It doesn't serve us when individuals, organisations or governments lose sight of other values in favour, simply, of beating the competition. It doesn't serve us when it drives us into the anxiety, stress and contractions that decrease our quality of life. The kind of scarcity mindset that competition can drive us into is no small matter. Experiments by behavioural scientists, Eldar Shafir and Sendhil Mullainathan, which are described by Rutger Bregman in his book, *Utopia for Realists*, show that when we are in financial scarcity, we actually make poorer decisions and score worse on cognitive tests. Any of you who, like me, have felt the difference between times when every expenditure has to be considered because every penny counts and times when we can spend freely will have a sense of this. The stress of financial scarcity can affect the quality of our thinking.

Given my experience and that of my clients, it seems clear that the negative effects of scarcity are not only present when it comes to our finances. A sense of scarcity can stop us taking sensible, rational decisions in all parts of our lives and false competition is a major source of that in our careers. The value of shifting out of the scarcity and into the possibility of our Higher Selves is clear.

We need to choose how we respond when we find ourselves in competition.

Be You

Sometimes, we will decide to compete. If we step out into the world to use our strengths in a marketplace, we will inevitably end up in some kind of competition. If we run a business, there will be other people who run similar businesses; if we do a job that requires our skills, there will be others who want the new role that we want. In these cases, *we can choose* the rules of engagement. As we learnt in Chapter One, most of the rules are invented anyway, so *we can choose* far more than we think.

In *You Are Unique*, branding coach, Eilen H. Klev, gives us good guidance on new assumptions to choose. She says that if you try to copy someone else's successes, strengths and experience, competition will feel hard. I would go further: if you are trying to compete with someone on their successes, strengths and experience, it will be physically and emotionally exhausting. It will be riddled with fear and contractions and stress and you probably won't win. Instead, if you want to avoid contractions and live more as your Higher Self as you use your strengths in the world, the wise option is to choose to compete based on *your* success, strengths and experience. Imagine being someone who saw what you do and tried to imitate it without the skills, experience and knowledge that are uniquely yours. Imagine being the poor person who tried to compete with you at being you.

Competing with the incredible corporate network of the other coach at the barbecue was, for me, riddled with fear and contractions. It was time to change the rules of competition that I was choosing.

Has the other coach at the barbecue spent thousands of hours of his youth acting, getting into characters and developing through that a deep understanding of other people's perspectives? I don't know, but I have.

Through his pursuit of acting and music, does he have an advanced practice of staying in the moment whilst holding onto structures, the core skill of a coach? I don't know, but I do.

Did the other coach spend years outside formal education, practising intuition and creativity more deeply than most children are ever given the chance to do? I don't know, but I did.

Did the other coach lead organisations, including one with hundreds of employees and a turnover of millions of pounds, before he even turned 30? I don't know, but I did.

Does the other coach come from a family of listeners, change-workers and spiritual practitioners that goes back generations? I don't know, but I do.

Imagine being the person who has to compete with that and remember: *no one can compete with you at being you.*

When we notice that the competition isn't real and choose instead to compete based on our own skills, experience and knowledge, new possibilities appear.

You can choose, for example, to compare yourself to who you were yesterday, not to who someone else is today, as the psychologist, Jordan Peterson, suggests in his book, *12 Rules for Life*.

You can focus on *being more you* this week than you were last week. On taking those strengths and gifts that only you have –

your Zone of Genius – and doubling down on it, knowing that not only does that open up our path to greater contribution and to our Higher Selves, but it makes us more likely to win our competitions.

Freed from false scarcity, focusing on comparing yourself to you yesterday and not to someone else today, you may see things in new ways. What if, for example, doing the same kind of work as your brother allows you to share all the things you have in common from growing up in the same family, opens up new ways to develop your relationship, and brings you closer together than you have been since you used to play computer games together on the cold landing of your childhood home?

Wouldn't that be nice?

And what about when you meet someone new who has a totally different network and a totally different skillset to you, but who is linked to you by a magical learning experience you have both been through? What if, instead of contracting into competing with them on their strengths, you notice that you both bring something special to this work and that you both have a commitment to changing the world, one person at a time? What can you give to each other? What can you learn? What can be created between you?

How Do I Do This?

Like many aspects of this book, this work requires thought and practice.

Perhaps the most important thing to remember is that you can only make your biggest possible contribution to the world by using the unique mix of skills and talents that *you* have.

My suggestion to you is this: make a commitment to understand your Zone of Genius – the unique mix of skills and experience that only you have – a little more every day. Then make a commitment to use it a little more every day, too. Not only is this a way to begin to compete with others on using the things that make you unique, but it is a vital component for each of us in making the biggest contribution we can in the face of the complex challenges of the modern world[6].

There are many ways to do this. Here are some starting points.

Gay Hendricks' book, *The Big Leap*, is where he coined the phrase 'Zone of Genius' to describe the set of activities each of us is uniquely suited to do: the sweet spot that brings together the things we love, the unique mix of talents and experience we have developed and the things that generate abundance and fulfilment for us. *The Big Leap* is full of questions and suggestions for how to understand your Zone of Genius. What do I love most to do? In my work, what produces the highest ratio of abundance and satisfaction to amount of time spent? When I'm at my best, what is the exact thing that I'm doing?

You can also take a strengths assessment like CliftonStrengths to identify your talents. Then use the expertly designed results and suggestions to find ways to use those strengths in your life and work. Gallup's research reveals that when people get to use their strengths every day, they are more engaged, more productive and report a better quality of life[7]. Simply becoming more aware of your strengths and talents and then using them more might see you reduce your feelings of stress and overwhelm. In particular, when you find yourself competing with someone on *their* strengths, remember yours and choose to use them.

Once you have found the things that make you unique and begun to bring them more into your work and life, however, the game will not be over. In fact, as I have explained already, when we care deeply about something – and it's hard not to care deeply about our unique abilities – we can face strong contractions and big challenges.

Remember that evolutionary fears may be at play, too, and that assumptions about scarcity and competition may be holding you back. The questions and ideas in this chapter can help you understand the fears you feel and rewrite false assumptions you discover. Our social fears, like being laughed at, being embarrassed or humiliated, being seen to fail, can be linked to deep evolutionary fears that trigger us into contractions that are no longer relevant today. Almost always, our social fears either won't come to pass or won't turn out to be nearly as bad as we fear. Don't believe them. They cause stress and anxiety unrelated to the reality of the world and they hold us back from giving our gifts. Take action instead[8].

For those moments where taking action feels most difficult, I want to offer you two exercises to help you to face down your moments of contraction around competition and to build a deep appreciation for the uniqueness that you are bringing to the world.

For the first exercise, imagine you are in a room with 100 other people with whom you might find yourself feeling in competition. These are probably others who work in your field or the field you are thinking of pursuing, but it could also be other people changing career, other single people, other parents and more. All 100 of you raise your hands in the air and someone at the front reads out statements. Anyone for whom each statement is true keeps their hand in the air; anyone for whom they aren't true takes theirs down. What are the statements that might be read out that would lead you to being the last person in the room with your hand in the air, making you unique among these 100 competitors?

This exercise helps us identify the qualities, beliefs and experiences that set us apart. We can then choose to compete with others on these things, rather than trying to fit ourselves into someone else's (real or imagined) list of qualities or experiences. This isn't always easy to do by yourself. If you want some help, you can find some suggestions for uncovering those things in a workshop and video series about creating a personal brand that expresses your uniqueness, which I made with my colleague Nicole Brigandi, available for free at www.robbieswale.com/mastering-your-personal-brand.

Once you have this list of statements about yourself, keep it. Read it when you doubt yourself or are scared. Put it on your website. Use it in the moments when you are struggling with contractions around competition.

In *This Is Marketing*, the marketing expert and author, Seth Godin, gives us a second exercise for times when taking action in the face of competition feels most difficult. Start by making a list of all the things that are desirable to the people you want to have an impact on (this might be your customers or clients, the people who manage promotions at work or another group). Then, imagine two axes, each labelled with one of the things from your list.

In business, people often slip into thinking they have to compete on price and convenience, and find themselves jostling for position with others in a race to be the cheapest and most convenient offer available. For most of us, however, that's the exhausting experience of copying someone else and competing on *their* strengths (and, unless we are the Amazon of our industry, we will almost certainly lose). Instead, *we can choose* to position ourselves on the things that make us unique. Don't slip into competing on price or convenience, or other people's strengths, or the things social media might suck you into competing on, but choose instead to label the axes so that you – perfectly imperfect you – end up out by yourself in the top right-hand corner of the graph and the rest are scattered around the other quadrants (see Figure 4). When you compete and market yourself from this position, it might just be that all your competition falls away. Build your brand on the combination of things that only you have.

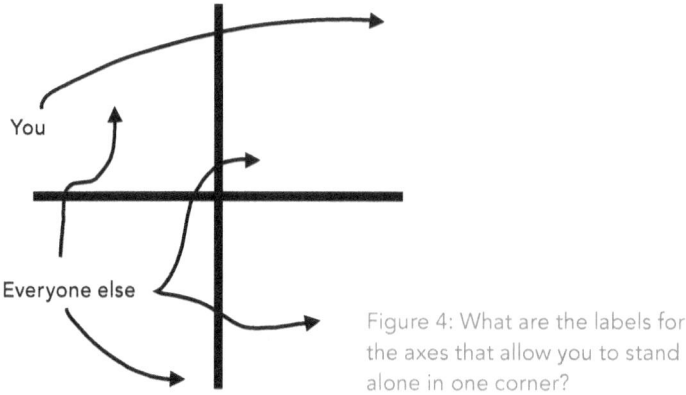

Figure 4: What are the labels for the axes that allow you to stand alone in one corner?

You can choose to compete or not to compete and *you can choose* what you compete on, so why not choose whatever competition is the most useful? More than that, why not choose whatever competition is the least stressful and most fun? Why not choose to compete at something that will reward you deeply on a quest to discover more about yourself and spend increasing amounts of time living as the person you want to be? That could be to compete at being the truest, best version of you. To paraphrase the psychologist and author, Robert Holden, what if the next level of success is available to you if you dare to be more fully who you really are?

The complexity of the 21st century is best faced with awareness of your uniqueness at your fingertips. To steady the ship we are all on together, the world needs you at your best, doing the work that only you can do. The world needs billions of people, competing to be the truest, best versions of themselves. That competition, with all of us competing to be the highest version of ourselves, might in fact be the only thing that can enable the human race to weather the storms of complexity we are experiencing today.

So, remember: no one can compete with you at being you.

And get to work.

CHAPTER FOUR SUMMARY

Key idea: Competition in the modern world makes acting as our Higher Selves particularly hard. The contractions we feel around competition can be based on a deep evolutionary fear triggered by caring about what we are working on and a false assumption that we must compete. What if *you can choose* to change the rules of the competition and shift to more useful assumptions? These could be that you don't need to compete at all or, where you do, that you can compete with others on the things that make you unique.

Ask yourself: *why do I need to compete with this person anyway?*
Remember: *no one can compete with you at being you.*

Exercises, practices and questions for reflection:

- **Dig into your fears to understand your Deeper Self.** Ask yourself, when you find yourself afraid: if this thing happens, then what am I afraid will happen next? When you have the answer, ask the question again. Keep asking it, going as deep as you can, to understand what this is *really* about.

- **Why do I need to compete with this person anyway?** Do I actually need to compete with this person? Does my success really depend on their failure?

- **Is competition serving me here?** Does the competition spur me on to new heights or hold me in inaction? If 'It's All Invented,' as we discussed in Chapter One, how could I invent a story that serves me better?

- When you feel contraction around someone who is similar to you in some way, **how are you trying (and failing, at a personal cost) to compete with them at what makes *them* brilliant?** Then get curious about yourself: what are the things *you* do brilliantly? Where are you almost impossible to compete with? What is the combination of things that only you have, that only you do?

- **Notice when fears and assumptions about competition collide.** When you find yourself feeling contractions around people you might be 'in competition' with, ask: what do I care about? What am I afraid of? What am I assuming? What is actually true here?

- **Compare yourself to who you were yesterday, not to who someone else is today.** Focus on *being more you* this week than you were last week. Focus on taking the strengths and gifts that only you have – your Zone of Genius – and doubling down on it, knowing that not only does that open up your path to greater contribution and to your Higher Self, but it also makes you more likely to win your competitions.

- **Make a commitment to understand your Zone of Genius a little more every day.** Then make a commitment to use it a little more every day, too. Not only is this a way to begin to compete with others on using the things that make you unique, but it is also a vital component for each of us in making the biggest contribution we can in the face of the complex challenges of the modern world.

- **Ask yourself Gay Hendricks' Zone of Genius questions.** What do I love most to do? In my work? What produces the highest ratio of abundance and satisfaction to amount of time spent?

When I'm at my best, what is the *exact thing* that I'm doing?

- **Take a strengths assessment like CliftonStrengths.** Use the expertly designed results and suggestions to find ways to use those strengths in your life and work. When you find yourself competing with someone on *their* strengths, remember yours and choose to use them.

- **Imagine you are in a room with 100 other people who you feel you are competing with.** All of you raise your hands in the air and someone at the front of the room reads out statements; if the statements are all true about you, you keep your hand in the air and if they aren't, you take it down. What are the statements that might be read out that would lead you to being the last person in the room with your hand in the air?

- **Position yourself based on your strengths.** Don't listen to what others tell you that you have to compete on, but choose instead to draw the axes of your positioning graph so that you end up out by yourself in the top right-hand corner. When you draw the lines of comparison to suit you, it might just be that all your competition falls away.

- **What if the next level of success is available to you if you dare to be more fully who you are?** What would you do then? How would you be more fully who you are in your life and in your work?

Further Reading and Learning

- *Sapiens* by Yuval Noah Harari

- *You Are Unique* by Eilen H. Klev

- *12 Rules for Life* by Jordan Peterson

- Take the CliftonStrengths assessment. This can be done via the book *Strengthsfinder 2.0* by Tom Rath or by visiting www.gallupstrengthscenter.com

- *The Big Leap* by Gay Hendricks

- My work with Nicole Brigandi on building a personal brand based on what makes you unique, including exercises to help you do that: www.robbieswale.com/mastering-your-personal-brand

- *This Is Marketing* by Seth Godin

- *Authentic Success* by Robert Holden

- *How to Start (a book, business or creative project) When You're Stuck* by Robbie Swale

CHAPTER FIVE

RELATIONSHIPS OF POSSIBILITY

The end of a relationship. That was the involuntary stop that shook me out of the patterns of my life and set me on the journey of discovery that led to this book. It felt incredibly significant to me at the time: I felt deep emotional loss as my stories about past, present and future crumbled. I wouldn't wish that kind of emotional impact on anyone else, but without it, I'm not sure if or when I would have seen so clearly the value of learning more about myself and the world.

Katherine Woodward Thomas is the therapist and bestselling author whose work came further into the public eye when Coldplay singer, Chris Martin, and actress, Gwyneth Paltrow, used her phrase 'conscious uncoupling' as their marriage ended. Woodward Thomas speaks about the release of energy that comes from a relationship break-up and how powerful and useful this energy can be for us if we are able to harness it. When I heard Woodward Thomas say that, I could suddenly see how I had harnessed the energy from my break-up. I had made a commitment to myself that something good should come of it and, in particular, that if it was in my power, I should never have to go through that kind of pain and upset again. Through harnessing the release of energy and making that commitment, I started to see the world differently and, as I did, the three core ideas of this book gradually became the fulcrum around which I transformed my view of the world.

Over the course of this chapter, I will introduce you to some of the ways in which you can practise the ideas in this book – *you can choose, what if everyone is doing their best?* and *curiosity is the antidote to contraction* – in your romantic relationships.

Our romantic relationships are one of a handful of places, alongside our close family relationships and following the call to make an impact in the world, where we are most often challenged to grow. These relationships are one of the places in which many of us will find ourselves contracting most powerfully and most regularly. At the same time, they can be where we learn most deeply what it really means to be human, what it really means to face all the challenges of our psychology. Almost all of us are drawn inexorably to create intimate, romantic relationships and, upon entering into those relationships, we are faced with our best and our worst times. We encounter the places where we find the most joy and the places where we are forced to face some of our deepest losses; our strengths and our flaws; our best qualities and our weaknesses. We get to experience the times when we see, reflected in the eyes of our loved ones, the deeper, glorious human who we so wish to be: our Higher Selves. We must also face the times when we see in their eyes the things we fear we might become.

I believe that our relationships have the potential within them to be the most magical part of our life's journey. Transforming our relationships can unlock for us incredible personal potential. Many of us don't have the relationship we want deep down and so haven't unlocked and experienced the full support and energy that a romantic relationship can provide. This support and energy can fuel us as we do our work in the world and it can enable us to withstand the pressures we face, spending more and more time as our Higher Selves. Not only that, but our romantic relationships offer an unparalleled opportunity to understand our Deeper Selves. *We can choose* to use our romantic relationships to understand ourselves more deeply and through that gain more access to the person we are on our best days. Lastly, for those of us who have children, improving our romantic relationship can have an enormous impact on the next generation, on the ability of our children and their children to move skilfully through their own relationships and to act more and more as their Higher Selves.

The ways we are wired as humans, individually and societally, prompt us to seek out a mate and tell us that romantic relationships are deeply important. So, for most of us, no matter how often we may tell ourselves rationally that we don't need someone else, the intimate relationships that take place on our journey form an integral part of our lives. Whether you have a partner now or not, the ideas in this chapter will, I hope, provide you with insights to support you in creating romantic relationships that empower and enliven you.

I am certainly not here to support a Hollywood view of romantic relationships, unhelpful in its fairy tale simplicity and unfit for the complexity of real life. Relationships are hard, as we have discussed throughout this book, and they take work.

If you desire a more fulfilling romantic relationship, it is possible if you are willing to commit to it and to your own growth. *You can choose* that and perhaps it is not as far away from you as you think.

How Did This Happen?

'How did this happen?' (or something similar) was the question that I found myself asking in the aftermath of my break-up.

We were nice people. We had loved each other. We had had fun together. We both had the qualities I thought were important to enable people to relate to each other: she was sensitive, kind and clever and, as far as I could tell, so was I. We had been mostly honest, even about difficult things. We had shared so much over almost a quarter of our lives and our whole post-university experience. We had worked together. We had grown together. We had fallen in love and we had been through so many things. Wasn't that enough? How did it end with two years of struggle and months of pain? How did this happen?

People try to help you at times like that. Sometimes they even succeed. One person who succeeded in helping me was a colleague, who recommended a book produced by the UK relationship charity, Relate. I think I read it partly because of the respect I had for the colleague, partly because I was desperate for something to help me answer the question 'How did this happen?' and partly because it had a great title: *Moving on: Breaking Up without Breaking Down*. As I read it, I came to a rather shocking realisation: there was an enormous amount about relationships that I didn't know. Worse still, it was out there in easily accessible books and it could be learned. I just hadn't learned it.

It was a moment, an insight, that created possibility for me: a chance to choose my own adventure, to take back control of my life. 'It doesn't have to be like this. *I can choose* to develop my understanding by reading books like this. I can learn and make my relationships different next time.' It brought an empowering sense of agency and it was a dreadful kind of agency, too, because it had been possible for *that* relationship to be different. I just hadn't done enough. I hadn't learned about these things and so, instead, the relationship was gone, lost forever. In its place, I was faced with pain and loneliness.

My perspective shifted. It was not just 'How did this happen?' Now it was also 'Never again.' With my new perspective, my ability to be successful in romantic relationships was something that I could work on and improve and I spent the next few years pursuing all kinds of learning. I read and re-read books; I listened and re-listened to audiobooks. I found free online resources and paid for others. I made myself have conversations with my friends and family even though this wasn't something that I (nor some of them) found easy. I even undertook a two-term introductory course to learn about couples counselling. I was struck by how little I and others seemed to focus on improving our romantic relationships, especially given their central place in our lives and societies. There was so much insight about relationships out there and it was practical, useful and wise, and yet I hadn't known that I could get much better at relationships through learning these things. Why hadn't I listened when people shared some of these ideas with me in the past? Why, given how important relationships are to almost everyone, everywhere, had there been no notable relationship education in my school or university? And why was so much of the education about relationships in our society focused on those already breaking or broken and not on empowering people to create the relationships that could fulfil them?

As I learned more about how to be successful in my relationships, I came in the end to believe three things. First, that there is enough insight about relationships available to us that, given certain conditions, no relationship has to end in the kind of pain mine did. Second, that, again given certain conditions, no relationship has to end at all. Third, that, given certain conditions, any and every relationship has the potential to be a place in which we grow as people together, enriching our lives, being more fulfilled and being able to live more as our Higher Selves. These are grand claims, but they are claims I believe. This possibility for our relationships is something *we can choose*.

The conditions needed to end those deeply painful break-ups and divorces, perhaps even to end divorce altogether, are not complicated. Simultaneously, they are not easy. You need to understand the idea that I learned through that break-up: that our ability to have successful romantic relationships is not fixed, that we can learn. The principles in Part One of this book will make a big difference, too, as you will see, but when you really boil it down, there may be just one condition that is fundamental, a condition that contains those principles and more. It gives me great satisfaction to say that that one condition is love.

In his seminal book, *The Road Less Travelled*, psychiatrist and author, M. Scott Peck, writes:

> "I define love thus: The will to extend one's self for the purpose of nurturing one's own or another's spiritual growth."

This is the first, most important and possibly only condition needed to create relationships of possibility that fulfil us and support us to grow into the highest versions of ourselves. To make my grand claims about the possibilities for our intimate relationships a reality, I believe that both people in a relationship need to make a 100% commitment to love in the way that Scott Peck defines it. It must be a commitment lived and acted on every day and, indeed, recommitted to every day in each moment of frustration, contraction or judgment about your partner and vice versa. Each time you slip, you must recommit: in this relationship, I will extend myself, whenever I can, as best I can, for the purpose of nurturing my spiritual growth, and that of the person I love.

Choose Love

This isn't easy. It isn't easy to make the commitment and it isn't easy to hold to it. It also isn't easy to elicit that commitment from your partner. That's OK, though, because while I do hold these somewhat grand beliefs about relationships, I also want to share with you another side: the smaller, less grand, more practical side. There are things you can do in everyday life, starting today, that can bring about significant changes in your relationships.

You can bring about these changes without requiring your partner to do anything or read anything. In fact, you might be astounded by what happens with your partner almost instantly when you change how *you* are. You can also bring about significant changes for yourself, for and around your future relationships, even if you don't currently have a partner. When you want to introduce these ideas to a partner, be gentle. Sometimes running excitedly to them with newfound ideas can be met with, at best, a sceptical response. If that happens, remember to assume that your partner is doing their best and that it might not be the right time for them to absorb new ideas. If you choose to be different in your relationship and find ways to be more and more your Higher Self, your partner will notice and they may even get curious.

Steven Pressfield is the author of many books about taking steps to beat what he calls our 'Resistance,' the force in each of us that holds us back from creating the things that we are being called to create. The only way to beat Resistance, according to Pressfield, is to 'turn pro' around the things we are called to, whether that is writing, a business, a project to become healthier or 'anything that derives from our Higher Selves.[1]' Pressfield is very clear that one of the most important areas where it is useful to be aware of our Resistance and the need to turn pro is in 'those acts which entail commitment of the heart.'

Turning pro starts very simply: one day, you decide to do it. *You can choose* to start, whenever you want. Then you work at it, every day, with the respect that any professional would give to their work. I realise now that this is what I did when I set out on the journey of learning about relationships. I decided to turn pro in my relationships, rather than acting as though I was happy to just 'see what happened' with this incredibly important part of my life. That was the amateur way.

That I needed to turn pro was a different message to what I seemed to have picked up from society, from Hollywood and from fairy tales. That message seemed to be that if you found the right person, it would all be easy: relationships either work because you've found your soulmate or they don't because you haven't and love is a thing that you are either in or you are out of and certainly not something that you have to commit to every day. The message seemed to suggest some mysterious formula that says 'yes, you two can be happy together' when you have advanced through a series of common stages in a relationship, like going out a certain number of times or perhaps living together. Once that had happened, so my story went, your job was done and you lived Happily Ever After. That wasn't how my relationships up to that point had gone, though. They had started off following that story, until, all of a sudden, they very much hadn't.

My new story was that *I can choose* to affect my relationships, to change them, to work at them, to improve them. Essentially, this was a shift from 'my relationships happen to me' to 'my relationships are created by me.' There is certainly language out there in the world that tells us that we have to work at relationships. Perhaps on an intellectual level, I knew that already, but, deep inside, I don't think I believed it. I thought, perhaps, that working at relationships was for people who had chosen badly, weren't very romantic or were just bad at relationships. Not for people like me, people like us. In some ways, this was society's story. In others, it was my story: a story too black-and-white to be fit for the complexity of real life.

Through shifting my view on relationships, what I learned was this: that through turning pro in my relationships, I would have the opportunity to love better, to create more joy and happiness for the person I was in relationship with and to be a better man.

I started to see romance as different to the 'Hollywood soulmate' story, too. Where's the fulfilment in getting lucky when the love of our life happens to get into a lift with us or walk into the bookshop where we work? Yes, the romance of those chance meetings is beautiful, but what have I really achieved if I stumble across a soulmate in a bar or a class or a workplace and then it's just the two of us strolling off into the sunset? For me, the fulfilment, the deep romance, comes from deciding every day to turn pro, to lean into my relationship with love, as well as I can in that moment. It comes from deciding every day to extend myself for the purpose of nurturing my own and another's spiritual growth. The romance and excitement come from the agency, hope and possibility that arise from the realisation that, by behaving differently, we can truly affect our relationships. We can make them more fulfilling and empowering and enriching than we had imagined, sometimes quickly and sometimes slowly over years or decades. That is the courageous, hero's journey. That's what matters to me and it matters far more than my wish that my life could be a little bit more like a movie.

When I told my friend, coach and psychotherapist, Mike Toller, how Pressfield says we turn pro by simply deciding to, Mike was reminded of another story. Someone, tearing their hair out in despair at their relationship, asked a loved one 'How do you stay married?' The loved one replied: 'You don't get divorced.'

You can choose. Every day.

This journey, the one I'm inviting you on in your romantic relationships, starts with another choice, too. Am I willing to love myself? Not just any kind of love, but the kind of love that Scott Peck defines. Am I willing to extend myself for the purpose of nurturing my spiritual growth and that of others? The words 'extend myself' are important here. Am I willing to stretch myself, to grow? Am I willing to change? Am I willing to become a different person through this relationship? Am I willing to make that commitment, even though it will sometimes be hard?

These are questions for you to consider carefully and not ones to be taken lightly. Are you willing to commit to your relationships being a journey of discovery, a journey with the purpose of nurturing your and others' spiritual growth? Are you willing to *choose* to see your relationship that way?

If you are, it will open up even more opportunities to learn more about the deep parts of you, to learn how to dance with them more skilfully and learn how to be more often the skilful, wise, noble higher version of you.

This is exactly the kind of growth this book is concerned with: the chance to develop our way of seeing the world so it is bigger, higher and more able to cope with what life throws our way.

Leaning Across the Divide

It is not easy to love in the way Scott Peck describes. It sometimes feels as though our whole selves are set up against it. We are desperate to *win*, perhaps, in some relationship 'competition' against our partner. We are desperate to be 'right.' We are desperate to stay as we are and hold on to our sense of self. We would rather protect that, protect ourselves, put the blame outside us. It can sometimes feel like walking into gale-force winds to gift someone (or ourselves) the kind of love that Scott Peck talks about.

I once heard John Gray, author of the influential book *Men Are from Mars, Women Are from Venus*, tell a story about this in a seminar. He was speaking about an experience of being upset with his wife.

'How dare she talk to me that way?' Gray had thought. 'I can't put up with this anymore. I feel like a prisoner trapped in this relationship.' This feeling would happen after an argument with his wife.

'In this place,' he explained in the seminar, 'I was kind of just stuck.' From here, Gray was facing the reality of 'desperate to win,' 'desperate to be right' and 'desperate to stay as you are.' It was a fixed position.

'You know,' a friend said to him when he told them about the situation, the upset and the feeling of being a prisoner, 'you could just go say you're sorry.'

'And yeah,' says Gray, explaining what he had learned. 'I could say that. And then everything would change.'

What would change is that, in that moment, he would put himself at risk. He would put his sense of self on the line and open up to the possibility that he might be wrong. By offering the vulnerability of 'I'm sorry,' he would be extending himself for his own spiritual growth and for the spiritual growth of his wife. Instead of the fixed place, the false assumptions of competition, the scarcity of winning and losing, possibility would appear.

Gray explained in the seminar that what he believes we are after, deep down, is to find and maintain connection with our partners – the kind of connection we felt when we fell in love, but can drift away from us over time. This kind of connection was clearly not present for him in those moments of 'How dare she talk to me that way?'

When we are locked in this kind of disagreement and blame, it can feel as though there is a gulf between us. The adventure of love – Scott Peck's kind of love – is to extend yourself in those moments for your own and your partner's spiritual growth. You have to make a shift in your stance. What Gray's friend had observed was that 'I'm sorry' is a way to make the shift. *We can choose* to stay disconnected, arguing and feeling trapped in the relationship. *We can choose* to stay wrapped up in the idea that we are a victim, offended and outraged by how unreasonable our partner can be or, instead, we can extend ourselves towards connection.

By the time I heard this story, I already trusted Gray's work, having experienced the value of the insights in his writing. In my head, though, considering it as I wrestled with his story, I found myself thinking: 'But what about when I'm actually right? What about when she *is* the one being unreasonable? Why should *I* be the one to apologise?' I thought this as I reflected on the story and I felt it when finding myself, inevitably, in those moments of struggle and disconnection in my relationship. 'I can't apologise,' went the furious thought, '*I've* got nothing to apologise for.' This thought would repeat again and again and again. As it did, the feeling of being trapped would grow and the struggle or disconnection would remain unresolved. And then, one day, I tried it.

'I'm sorry.'

It was hard to say it and mean it, but I did. As Gray said, everything changed.

I felt different. My wife's disposition shifted. As I continued to practise saying 'I'm sorry' at these times, the shifts continued to happen. She would often apologise, too. Sometimes one of us would need to say it more than once before it could settle into the other person, but when it did, connection would return.

And I realised that if I am committed to extending myself for the purpose of nurturing spiritual growth for me and my partner, if I am committed to love, then being the one to lean in first with a phrase like 'I'm sorry' is something I need to commit to every day. If we both commit to this, then, far more often, we will move towards connection rather than away from it; far more often, at least one of us will find the skill in the moment to lean across the divide.

How can we say 'I'm sorry' and actually mean it, though? How can we do that if we have a commitment to honesty, to telling the truth when it matters? Well, we can say it because, in an argument in a romantic relationship, it is almost always both people's fault. Even when it seems far more one person's fault, we can be sorry for the loss of connection between us in that moment, for the sense that two people who care for one another are causing each other pain. We can remember that what we are doing as we fight against our desire to win, to be right, is that we are extending ourselves to nurture our spiritual growth and that of our partners. We can be sorry that, in the moment before saying 'I'm sorry,' we weren't acting from love.

The alternative to making that shift is to be held, contracted, in the importance of being right. In that moment, we have our hands held up, as in the demonstration from Fred Kofman's video that I discussed in Chapter Two. We are each pushing against the other person, determined to be right. Perhaps our nervous system is in the defensive state we discussed earlier in this book, rather than the social engagement state where we can be curious and relate to each other. Before we know it, both of us are pushing partly just because the other person is pushing. In some instances, years can pass like this, until no one can even remember who pushed first or why. The right words in those moments, like 'I'm sorry,' have the potential to turn the shoving match into a dance. They invite the other person, as their Higher Self, the adult they are deep inside, back into the relationship. They allow the contraction, which is driven by a desire for safety from some early or evolutionary memory, to release. They open up possibility again.

Saying 'I'm sorry' against our contraction, sacrificing the part of us that wants to be right for the good of the relationship, is admitting vulnerability and requires courage. It is certainly an act of extending ourselves for our and another's growth.

In my speech at my wedding, one of the things I spoke about was a series of moments when I know most of all that I am blessed with a wife who loves me deeply. These are not the moments of joy and happiness. They are not Hollywood moments of flowers or candles or celebration, although those are wonderful moments, too. The moments when I know most of all that she loves me as deeply as I could ever want are the moments when Emma is furious, angry or upset with me. Often, it is because I have done something quite infuriating. Sometimes, I am 'right' and of course sometimes Emma is 'right.' Sometimes both of us are, sometimes neither. I feel her love the most in those moments when she is able to turn, despite her contraction, and extend herself towards me across the divide between us. Often, she does this by saying, 'I'm sorry.'

Seeing someone taking that incredibly courageous and vulnerable step is inspiring. Having witnessed that courage, I have felt myself, many times, being drawn from the shoving match into the dance. It is hard to resist the pull of that kind of apology, that kind of love. If you have made the commitment to love as we are defining it in this chapter, then it is almost impossible to resist the pull when someone says those words to you. Instead, the words come, sometimes easily and sometimes with difficulty, and you say 'I'm sorry, too.' Sorry, at least, that the two of you have lost connection in that minute, hour or day.

I believe this is one of the fundamental differences between relationships that last and relationships that don't. If both people are willing to try to lean in towards the other person, to extend themselves across the divide, then over the months and years, these people will grow and develop in their love together. They will be nourished by their relationship and they will recapture the feeling of falling in love, as John Gray says. If they are not willing, then there may come a time when the relationship will be stretched too far,

Relationships of Possibility

when the divide will feel too great to cross and someone will bring it to an end. This is the risk we run every time we do not dance with our partners enough to lean across the divide; this is what 'I'm sorry' can help to prevent.

'I'm sorry' is a practical and simple (but not always easy) way for you to begin to extend yourself to nurture your and another's spiritual growth. In relationships where the divide may have grown large, especially over a long period, it may be even more important to start with 'I'm sorry' and it may feel even more difficult to do so. It isn't always pleasant but taking these difficult and courageous decisions is exactly what it means to extend yourself.

You can start here, right now, if you feel ready: make a commitment, by yourself or with your partner, to loving in this way. If you aren't sure if you are willing to make this commitment yet, read on. You will understand this commitment with more context over the rest of this chapter and perhaps by the end you will find yourself willing to make the commitment. Perhaps you will find other ideas or concepts easier to initiate. If you try something else and find it makes a difference, come back to this commitment of love.

Once you have made the commitment to Scott Peck's definition of love, you will find yourself in a different relationship. Here is what you may find: suddenly the arguments, the disagreements, the times you find yourself triggered and contracting take on a different frame. Instead of being clear signs that love is absent, that this person isn't 'the one,' that this person has never and will never 'really get you,' each struggle and trigger is an opportunity to express love. Each is an opportunity to get curious and follow that curiosity into and through your contractions. It is an opportunity to grow and develop, to find your way to your Higher Self and to give yourself the resources you need to change the stories that are holding you back. Each is an opportunity to give these gifts to someone you love.

Towards the end of this chapter, I will come back to some of these ideas about why it is vital for us to transform our relationships, to look for developmental opportunities and work through them. Before that, I will describe several more ideas that have helped me to spend less time contracting and more time in connection in my relationship. These are ideas that have helped me to extend myself for my own growth and the growth of the woman in my life.

We Are Different

I wonder if an unintended consequence of the fight for equality between the sexes is that many parts of our society have subconsciously (or consciously) fused the idea of men and women being 'equal' with the assumption that men and women are 'the same.' At the very least, this was an assumption I held and it undoubtedly held back my relationships. When I began to change that assumption to a new one – that the fight for equality of opportunity for men and women was vital, but that the fundamental, important and beautiful differences between the sexes were real and worth celebrating – it had an enormous effect on the success of my relationships.

We can think of the changing attitudes to the equality (or not) and similarity (or not) between men and women as a series of shifts in assumption, from so simple they were oppressive (with traditional gender roles), to far less simple but still too simple for the complexity of actual relationships ('men and women are equal' confused with 'men and women are the same'), to something more ready for the real world (which might just shift everything in your relationship).

The need for the collective and individual assumption that men and women are 'the same' comes as a reaction to some of the truly oppressive parts of our cultures that we have thankfully mostly left behind. Today, many of the broad assumptions that society seems to have held about things that women 'couldn't' do seem incredible, whether about voting, serving in the armed forces or serving in parliament. Having watched the explosion of achievements from women since those assumptions were changed in law, it's clear that the assumptions were far too simple for the reality of humans.

In the quest for equal rights for women, which continues today, fought across the world by courageous people, came a determination that women should not be treated any differently to men. 'Men and women should be treated the same' is clearly a more complexity-fit assumption than from whatever oversimplistic ideas the oppression of women emerged. This new assumption of equality was a value I grew up with and, in many places in society and in modern life, it is only a wonderful, empowering thing. However, one of the places where, for me at least, this beautiful quest for equal rights had a darker shadow was in my romantic relationships.

Could it be that things aren't as simple as 'men and women should be treated the same'? Could it be that that is an assumption that needs to be transcended and included to build a new viewpoint, fit for the complexity of the world we live in?

Treating women as though they were exactly the same as men hid from me the possibilities that are available when we truly acknowledge our differences. It has been fundamental to the growth of fulfilment in my relationships to acknowledge and grow to understand how we are not the same. Not only has it enabled me to love and support my wife in a completely different way, supporting her better and arguing and fighting less often, but it has enabled me to understand myself more deeply as a man, seeing more clearly the times when my uniquely masculine qualities are at play. We, men and women, must hold equally important places in society – we are thankfully far closer to this across the world than we were a hundred years ago – but we are not the same. Our biology is different, in everything from our sexual organs to our bone structure and our hormonal make-up. The ways our minds work are different, too.

Seeing and then acting with awareness of the differences between men and women has far-reaching consequences. At its core, it enables us to understand each other's perspectives with more skill: it makes engaging the key idea of Chapter Two, *what if everyone is doing their best?*, far easier. I can see how my wife is doing her best because I now acknowledge that she may be doing things because she sees some aspects of the world fundamentally differently to how I see them. I can also be more patient if she finds me frustrating because I understand that she finds it equally challenging when I see things differently to how she does.

Many of the writers and teachers whose work on romantic relationships I have explored hold the differences between men and women at the centre of their work. Gray's *Men Are from Mars, Women Are from Venus*, for instance, tries to help people understand the differences between women and men by offering us an assumption to choose: what if the other person were an alien, from a different planet to you? Gray essentially gives people an extra perspective that makes it far easier to ask *what if everyone is doing their best?*

I won't explore all of the authors whose work has influenced my thinking here, but I will give some practical examples to begin to show you some of these differences between men and women and to give you some places to start. I will illustrate the work of these experts with stories from my life and relationships, but I want to make it clear that this isn't just about my experience. Each of the experts I will speak about here have based their ideas on decades of work and research and each of these patterns I identify here are ones I have seen and discussed elsewhere with family, friends and clients.

Relationships of Possibility

Gender has become a charged and politicised topic in recent years, so before I go further, I want to make several things clear. First, I am not suggesting that all men or all women are identical in their preferences, their hormonal make-ups or their physiology. Indeed, as Gray says in his 2017 book, *Beyond Mars and Venus*, each of us has a unique mix of masculine and feminine qualities and one of the possibilities in modern relationships (freed from the stereotypes of the past) is for each of us to express those unique mixes. This has more than an echo of the ideas of Chapter Four: that our aim should be to express our unique mix of abilities, skills and experience and that, by doing that more fully, we might find our next level of success. However, even with all that in mind, the males and females of species across nature are most certainly different from each other. Humans are no exception.

Secondly, clearly not everyone engages in a female-male relationship. In this chapter, I will sometimes write explicitly about female-male relationships: this is where my personal experience lies and sharing ideas and insights I have tested in my own life is a fundamental part of this book. If you don't engage in female-male relationships, some parts of this chapter may be less useful than others; indeed, given the many different kinds of romantic relationships that exist in a free society, I suspect each of us will find different parts more powerful than others. Whether you engage in female-male relationships or not, whatever your gender and whatever your personal, unique mix of masculine and feminine qualities, I believe and hope that the insights contained in the following pages have the potential to support you to create more fulfilling romantic relationships. Whatever romantic relationships you engage in, the stories and ideas in this chapter may give you the opportunity to understand yourself and the people around you more deeply.

Acknowledging and understanding the differences between men and women has been completely transformational for me. I hope the same may be true for you. Over the rest of this chapter, I will speak about some of those differences and how they have impacted my life and those I love. Of course, *you can choose* which ideas you take and apply.

'I Love You,' Dragon Slaying, the Toilet Seat and the Shopping Bags

I don't remember the exact moment I first said, 'I love you.' I do remember that it was with my first university girlfriend. I was probably 19. I remember realising I did love her, realising that what I was feeling was, in fact, the feeling of being in love. And I remember that saying it to her felt enormous. Wow. I'm in love.

I was caught entirely off guard a few weeks later when we had a big argument. The crux of it was this: she didn't feel like I loved her. In my head, I was gobsmacked: 'How can you possibly think that?! I told you I did. I said these enormous words, for the first time ever.' I felt hurt. Did she not realise how important and significant it was to me to say that, especially for the first time? Did she not believe me, not trust my word? Somehow, over that conversation or a following one, I came to realise that it wasn't that she didn't trust my word. It was that she didn't think like I did. For me, once I had said 'I love you,' I loved her. As far as I was concerned, she could safely assume that I loved her until the day I told her, 'I don't love you.' I've said it once, which means it's clear and settled.

It was different for her, though. She felt I hadn't expressed my love enough and so she felt unloved and upset. This was the last thing I wanted, so to avoid this (and the arguments that followed),

I needed to try something different. Here's what I came up with: every time I felt the feeling that I associate with being in love – for me, it's a kind of rising feeling similar to excitement in my chest or sometimes it's the tingling of sweet tears at my eyes and nose – I would say 'I love you.' We never had that fight again and it is a practice I have carried through my subsequent relationships and into my marriage.

At the time, I didn't understand where that misunderstanding had come from; I simply saw it and found a way around it. Years later, when I read *Men Are from Mars, Women Are from Venus*[2], I saw much more about what had been going on and found myself with so much more choice in my relationships. In that book, John Gray writes about what leads to men and women feeling loved by their romantic partner. Often men and women fall into confusing traps through believing the opposite sex sees things the same way that they do. Gray uses the metaphor of a points system, where we score our romantic partner, mostly subconsciously, with points in proportion to the amount of love we feel in response to their behaviour. According to Gray's work, women, on the one hand, tend to believe that it is the number of things they do for a man that makes the difference for him, but instead it is *the way she acts and feels* when she does those things that fills him up with love. Men, on the other hand, work hard to do things for their romantic partners and believe that women score them based on the size of the task the man has done. Instead, size doesn't matter. In a woman's points system, Gray says, anything a man does for a woman equals one point. Holding the door open, one point. Doing the washing up, one point. Paying the rent on time, one point. Picking the kids up, one point. Working all hours to get promoted to pay for the new house, one point. Slaying a dragon, one point. Making dinner, one point.

So, whilst a man may do something that he thinks is incredibly significant (perhaps saying 'I love you' for the first time in his life), for a woman, this will still only equal one point. And this *really matters* because these points are what a woman needs to feel loved. At 19, I didn't say 'I love you' any more after that first time because I genuinely didn't know that it mattered to my girlfriend. I had said it, once, and that felt enormous, like slaying a dragon. I thought, subconsciously, that this would give her the enormous dragon-slaying amount of love that I felt. I thought she would be just like me, which felt like a pretty safe assumption, especially with my 'men and women are the same' assumption. I knew she loved me because she had said it. And I felt loved. So, given I had said I loved her, she must feel loved, too.

As soon as I understood that it did matter to her, though, I was able to adjust, filling her up with love and making her happier. Essentially, I realised that I could get one point, each one filling her up with more and more love, by saying 'I love you' every time I felt it. That felt like a really good deal.

Many years later, I notice myself using this insight in all sorts of places, as I have learned with my wife what makes her feel loved (and earns me points). I don't even know how much she specifically notices the things that I do, but I know that they are working. They are all things that, to me, seem a little irrational, but I have learned to trust that they matter just as much to her as my making a success of my business or helping us buy a house. Not rationally as much, at least to me, but equally as much if my goal is for her to feel loved.

I maintain the practice of communicating my love verbally every time that it crosses my mind or my heart, either in person or with a text message or email, but there are other things, too. No matter how inefficient it sometimes seems to me to make the bed (we're only going to unmake it when we get in it again in the evening), leave her bedside light on if she's home after I'm asleep (turn it on yourself...what about the electricity bill?) or how rationally unfair it is that I have to put the toilet seat down but she doesn't have to put it up (where are equal rights now, eh?!), I know that these little things and others matter to Emma and I know that she will feel loved that little bit more when I do them. So, I do them. There are other less 'irrational' things that make a difference, too. For example, it seems apparent that if I get a glass of water for Emma and put it on her bedside table before she gets there, she feels incredibly loved. That kind of thing doesn't make much difference to me, but as a man, once you understand the system of points that women use, then it makes so much sense to do these things. If this thing I can do, whether something practical like making the bed or something more traditionally romantic like buying flowers for no reason, makes her feel the same amount of love as the big gestures that I think matter much more, then suddenly making the bed seems an incredibly efficient way to score more points (or, if you prefer, to give my love to my wife).

Of course, these are examples from our relationship. Some women may not care about the bedside light being on and some men may be fastidious about making the bed, but the key principle here is to think carefully about what small things you can do to make a difference for the woman in your life.[3]

I learned early in our relationship the power of doing the small things for Emma when, staying at her flat in London, we went to the supermarket. As we left, I offered to carry the shopping; not my fair share, but all of it. I had read Gray by then, so I might even have been thinking of showing her I loved her in this way. Emma let me and it is a story she still tells about our relationship. She felt loved in that moment and, as she walked away from the supermarket unburdened by the bags, she felt the absence of another weight: she didn't have to shoulder the burden of everything in her life alone. She could rely on me and be loved by me. Now, I try to carry the shopping whenever we shop together, safe in the knowledge that it will help her feel loved, both in that moment (yes, one point!) and by reminding her of another moment, years ago, when more than one weight was lifted.

The shopping bags story also demonstrates another part of the difference Gray describes. One of the ways a man feels loved is by being appreciated, by feeling that he can make a difference and by being able to help. Just as a gift men can give to women is to *do the small things*, a gift women can give to men is to *allow them to help*. This is all the more significant now because of the amazing leaps we have made towards equality in recent years. Most women (in countries like the UK, at least) don't practically need men outside of reproduction (and maybe not even there). Women reading this, especially of my generation and younger, may earn more than the men in their lives and probably know how to do everything practical that used to be the preserve of men, such as changing a tyre or fiddling with the radiators. Many of us men don't know how to do those things anymore either!

So, just as making the bed, saying 'I love you' every time one feels it or buying spontaneous flowers can be simple ways for a man to show a woman in his life that he loves her (even if he thinks this is a little nonsensical compared to the dragon-slaying he may have been up to), so can you make a man in your life feel loved in ways a woman might find nonsensical. You can do this by letting him help (even if we all know you can carry the shopping yourself) and by appreciating him for the help he gives.

The story of the shopping bags stays with me because – and this is the total, honest truth – in that moment, I felt like a hero from a story. This woman, this amazing woman who I admire for all her courage and her success and her charm and her beauty, needs me.

In that moment of her appreciation, which I later realised I had felt starved of at the end of my previous relationship, I felt like I really had slayed a dragon. And all it took was for her to let me carry the shopping and then explain from the heart that it helped. It was a small thing and yet the way she felt as she expressed her gratitude was so pure and loving that I gave her many points in exchange for the huge rush of love and appreciation I felt.

This experience supports what Gray suggested in 1992 when *Men Are from Mars, Women Are from Venus* was first published: that it is the way a woman acts and feels towards a man that affects how many points of love he will feel from something she does for him, rather than the size of the task or the task itself. If a woman secretly resents a man, it doesn't matter how significant a thing she does is, the man will feel little love and so she will receive few or no points. If she deeply loves and appreciates him, it doesn't matter how small or large the thing she does for him is, she will receive many points. For women, what this means is that if you want to fill up your man with love, look for, notice and find your genuine appreciation for him and who he is and what he does. Appreciate him honestly every time you can.

Focus and Awareness

After we had been together for maybe three years, I introduced Emma to one of my favourite television shows. *Six Feet Under* follows the Fisher family and their funeral home. It is a beautiful and emotive examination of life through the prism of death and grief.

As we sat in our flat watching perhaps the most emotive scene of all seven seasons, somewhere towards the end, Emma got up and took the dinner plates from the coffee table to the kitchen.

Mid-scene! At the emotional climax of a show that is based almost entirely on creating brilliant, emotional climaxes! I couldn't believe it. I was so upset I switched off the TV and refused to watch the rest of the show. I was hurting, in my chest, in my heart. This show was important to me. It was something that I wanted to share with her. All I could think was that the only reason I would have even noticed the plates was if the show was incredibly boring. So boring, in fact, that I was sitting looking around wondering what would be more interesting than this over-emotional, indulgent nonsense. The idea that Emma was thinking this was deeply upsetting.

I was triggered. I contracted. I judged Emma swiftly and I acted from that place, hurt and confused. I lashed out verbally, hurting and confusing her in the process.

I wasn't as skilful in my ability to dance with my contractions then as I am now and I wasn't as practised at playing with *what if everyone is doing their best?*, but even if I had been, I don't think at that time in my life I would have been able to understand how she could possibly have been doing her best.

What later brought me to a deeper understanding was Emma's engagement with the work of Alison Armstrong, a teacher, writer and educator who has spent several decades studying men and women. At this point, Armstrong's work had already had a significant impact on me, but Emma's engagement with it, as part of her commitment to love, to extending herself for the growth of herself and of me, gave us a common language to use as we navigated our differences. Like Gray's, Armstrong's work is based on the discoveries she made through her research into the ways that men and women see and experience the world differently. Like Gray, Armstrong places deep importance on the way women and men don't realise the extent of their differences. She says that men tend to treat women as soft, more lovely, emotionally indulgent men, while women tend to treat men as misbehaving, hairy women. She says that, by understanding more accurately the different ways we experience the world, we can see when our partner's behaviour is in some way about us, for instance, hating a television programme we hold dear, and when it is just something about how she or he is. The difference at play in this example, and one that Emma and I still find ourselves navigating, is a difference in the way the attention of men and women works.

Men have what Armstrong calls Single Focus Awareness. For me, this shows up like this: if I am watching something, that is all I am doing. I am unaware of most of the other things that are going on around me. Sometimes I am so engrossed in what I am doing that I don't even hear when Emma says something to me. It's not that I don't listen, I don't *hear*. Or, I hear, but in a totally subconscious way that I only notice when Emma calls it to my attention (often with frustration at the impoliteness of my seemingly ignoring her). When I dig into my subconscious, sensing her frustration or upset, I sometimes realise that on some level I heard the question, judged if it really needed a response, decided it didn't (especially while my valuable attention is on something 'more important') and so didn't answer. If I'm lucky, I can sometimes answer the question belatedly or at least say 'I'm sorry' before the silence gets too long.

I do all that, somehow, without noticing or thinking about it. I may also not notice the time or forget to check my phone even when expecting an important call or message. I sometimes get so focused on a task, for instance, on getting the printer to work, that I forget that there might be a much better and more effective way of getting to the goal I am working towards (printing something). Maybe it's emailing it to a neighbour to print or printing it another day in an office, but I don't think of that, lost as I am in my Single Focus Awareness.

An example that Armstrong gives about this is of men (including me) who sit and flick through 100 channels on the TV before declaring, 'There is nothing on.' Clearly, there are lots of things on, but what a man really means when he says that is, 'My attention is finite and focused. It is a gift for me to give it to something, it is a significant investment for me, and so I will only give it to things I feel are worthy of it.'

The flip side of the Single Focus Awareness in my experience is that, when my focus is broken, it feels almost like an invasion or a violation. It's almost painful. Moving my attention often – interrupting it, then refocusing, then interrupting, then refocusing – is exhausting. Whilst activity by myself, such as watching sport or reading, is often regenerative and nourishing for me, dragging my attention away and putting it back is instead draining, tiring and irritating.

When engrossed and deeply focused on something that is very important to me, like watching *Six Feet Under*, the disruption caused by Emma getting up was a shock to my system. Not only that, but it was impossible for me to understand how she could even notice the plates unless she had decided, as I might with 100 channels, that it just wasn't a programme worth watching.

I can imagine these last few paragraphs might seem very alien to the women reading. I know this because it is so difficult for me to understand the way that a woman's attention works, which is, in Armstrong's language, Diffuse Awareness. It is so difficult for me, in fact, that I am going to use Armstrong's words to explain.

"The easiest thing, guys, is to think this is a version of how *you* think," Armstrong says in her audiobook/workshop, *Understanding Women*. "It's NOT. 'Diffuse' means to pour in every direction. As a man, you are Single Focused. You pay attention to one result at a time. We have Diffuse Awareness. Most men will interpret this as 'Oh, so you pay attention to three or four results at a time?'

Noooo. 'Oh, you focus on two or three things at a time?' Nooooo. It means *we don't focus*."

Armstrong, along with many others who do work about the differences between men and women, often uses humour to get her points across. When handled with love as she does, there certainly seems to be something funny in the surprising and stark differences between men and women. She gets a big laugh at this point in the workshop. We all know that women are able to focus. So, what is she really saying here?

"We don't focus," she repeats. "It doesn't mean we can't focus, because we can," she says, before going on to explain with great humour and affection that it takes the same amount of energy for her to focus for long periods as it does to get a shuttle out of the atmosphere.

Diffuse Awareness. Pouring in every direction. So, whilst for me it is impossible to focus on *Six Feet Under* and the dishes at the same time, Emma's awareness is picking up the dishes and *Six Feet Under* and probably about a million other things going on in that moment. Not only that, but sometimes, Emma says, it is as though the things in her Diffuse Awareness are speaking to her or shouting or even screaming at her. The screaming won't stop, in the example in our story, until the plates are moved away. She also explains that unlike me, she can still have the same amount of awareness of the television programme whilst carrying the plates to the kitchen. At this point, suddenly I can understand why she might need to get up. I can see how she is doing her best; I can get out of judgment, out of how I think things 'should be,' and see them as they are. As is so often the case when we answer the question 'How is this person doing their best?', everything about the situation looks different. I can forgive her the hurt of her 'ignoring' the show, which I can suddenly see isn't what she has done, and *I can choose* to be more patient in future, avoiding the tantrum of switching off and getting upset.

With this knowledge and understanding, that the differences between us are so much more distinct than we had realised, Emma and I are able to reach across the divide more often and more skilfully (often with 'I'm sorry'). It doesn't mean that we don't have fights, that we don't upset and frustrate each other, because we do. What it means is that we can be our Higher Selves more: nimbler and more skilled at reaching out across the divides; repairing, recovering and rediscovering that feeling of being in love. Ending our days at peace with ourselves more often, not wrapped up in 'being right' or what should have been.

With this knowledge, we can dance out of contraction and create more possibility in our relationship. And you can, too.

The Deepest Possibility

The first people I heard speaking about the idea of an end to the ending of relationships were writers and therapists (wife and husband), Helen LaKelly Hunt and Harville Hendrix. Speaking as part of the *Art of Love* interview series in 2014, they said they believed that we now have the insights, tools and techniques to end divorce. Speaking powerfully about the branch of therapy, Imago, which they had designed, they showed me again that relationships aren't just something to get into and then see where they go. We have much more of a part to play than that. *We can choose* to behave in certain ways and, if we do, then perhaps we can create a relationship that doesn't end.

My previous assumption had been that those of us alive today might be living in the dark age of long, committed relationships. It's no wonder I felt that way, given we are so often told statistics about how many marriages end in divorce[4]. As I heard Hunt and Hendrix's vision, my previous assumption was replaced by possibility: we might instead be in the age where everyone has access to the tools to create the relationships that, deep down, their souls are craving. This is another *you can choose* moment: as with the optical illusion or the student in Ben Zander's class in Chapter One, we can try on each of these stories. We can see how we feel with each of them; we can see which makes our life better or empowers us more in our relationships. And then *we can choose.*

In Hendrix's book, *Getting the Love You Want*, he unpacks further the ideas of Imago therapy. Not only does he believe that, by doing certain things and behaving in certain ways, we can end divorce, Hendrix believes that our relationships, at their very core, are a mechanism by which we can heal the scars of our childhoods. We can use our relationships to see the patterns and coping mechanisms we have developed and, by working through these, give ourselves an increasing ability to access our Higher Selves. In the language of this book, our relationships are at their very core a mechanism for understanding our Deeper Selves. The scars we carry are often memories that leave us triggered, both in our relationships and outside. They are patterns and ways of behaving in the world that we subconsciously bring with us everywhere we go. They are the outdated safety mechanisms that keep us cooped up, hiding away, contracted and held back from our Higher Selves. They are what keep us from the things we can achieve, do and create in the world.

In Hendrix's book, he shows beautifully (and sometimes painfully) how the patterns we learn about relationships from our parents or primary caregivers, healthy or otherwise, influence enormously how we relate to others. This was something I had learned about myself as I used *curiosity is the antidote to contraction*. It is a frame you can use, too: look at the patterns in your romantic relationships and the patterns and relationship experience of your parents or caregivers.

Where do the patterns overlap? Where are they surprisingly, sometimes extraordinarily, similar? As we look for partners, explains Hendrix, we look for someone who it seems to us will be so different from the parent we most wish had been different: the one who didn't love in the way we needed or could have been 'better.'

However, each of us – you, me, our potential partners – finds ways to disguise our struggles and compensate for our areas of weakness by developing coping mechanisms. So, what we see in our partners as we select them is not everything, not the whole person, but mostly the person's ways of coping with their struggles, scars and the ways they were let down as a child or adolescent by their caregivers. Throughout the course of a long-term relationship, we gradually see through the coping mechanisms to the scars, struggles and truth of our partners, to their Deeper Self. There, instead of being as different from the mother or father we didn't want to end up with, we find ourselves with someone almost *exactly* suited to pushing our buttons, pressing our scars, triggering our hurts and wounds. We find ourselves in a relationship that is exactly what we hoped to avoid.

We can decide to leave these relationships when we see this and find someone different instead, but, as Hendrix asserts, we will simply subconsciously seek out this kind of person again and continue to find ourselves face-to-face with our patterns and struggles. This is why we see ourselves (or perhaps it's easier to see it with our friends) ending up with a series of partners who have so much in common in the way they let us down or fail to live up to our expectations. Each one seems different at first, only to end with a sometimes uncannily similar outcome.

Assuming our relationships work like this doesn't sound like an adventure that we would want to choose, but it can be. This is because choosing the adventure Hendrix describes gives us an incredibly deep opportunity for love, the kind of love that Scott Peck describes. *We can choose* to extend ourselves for the spiritual growth of ourselves and our partner, to realise that only by bringing ourselves face-to-face with someone who is able to trigger and activate our old learned hurts and patterns can we heal ourselves. Similarly, only by our partner coming face-to-face with us, the person who is able to trigger and activate their old learned hurts and patterns can they heal themselves. And what possibility lies here, then, in the darkest moments of our relationship, in the deepest struggles?

It is not that we are broken or flawed or are a fool for having chosen the wrong person. It is not that we are doomed to repeat the same patterns as our mothers and fathers and their mothers and fathers, as we may have already done many times in our life. It is instead that, by facing these moments, by dancing through them accompanied by our loving partner, we can truly grow into the person we have the capacity to be. We can break patterns that may have been passed down for generations, heal unhealthy parts of the lineage of which we are part. We can do this *only* by learning from the most difficult moments of our relationships, with someone selected almost perfectly to push our buttons, and by bringing curiosity as the antidote to our contraction in these most difficult of moments, where we feel so exposed in front of the person who matters the most. By doing that, we can find our way through to the openness we require and the possibility that awaits.

In each dark moment, where we look at ourselves and realise that we have chosen what we thought we didn't want in a partner, we can awaken to the possibility that only together can two people as flawed as you and I heal through love. Only together can we heal our deepest wounds and create the deepest possibilities for our lives together. Only together can we unlock those parts of our Deeper Selves and free ourselves to live as our wise, skilful, noble Higher Selves.

That is an adventure worth choosing.

Beginnings and Endings

This idea, from Hunt and Hendrix's work, is one of the biggest ideas in this book. It raises questions around who we choose as our romantic partners and when and why we might bring our relationships to an end. That final message – that only together can two people as flawed as you and I heal – carries so much. It is an empowering message that allows me to hold onto love at the times when I feel the most fears: that I have chosen wrongly, that I am trapped, that I should give up and run. I bring this idea to you now so that, if you want to, *you can choose* to believe this, too. It may help you hold onto love at the times that feel most difficult.

I know, for some of you reading this, that questions will be arising about your relationships. Could I have saved that one that ended tragically? Am I discovering my partner is bad for me? Or you might be asking questions about my relationships. Had I known what I know now, for instance, could a previous relationship have survived? Would I then have missed out on the marriage I am in? All I can speak to, to answer these questions, is my experience.

I have no doubt that if I had known then what I know now, my previous relationships would have been much better. Maybe some could have survived, through increased knowledge, skill, nimbleness and love. Maybe they could have flourished.

What matters most, though, right now, is a choice: if I can improve this relationship I am in, through learning new things, through loving differently, do I choose to? Do I want to put that effort in? Am I willing to commit to Scott Peck's definition of love?

There, in those questions, lies freedom, choice and responsibility; there lies 'my relationship is created by me' and not 'my relationship is happening to me.'

So, how do we use that responsibility?

As we discussed in Chapter Three, freedom can feel dreadful. The weight and pressure of those choices, that responsibility, can be hard to bear. Each of us is faced with the complex maze of our lives: a diversity of priorities unique to us, a diversity of values that matter. In moments of complex choice, especially around our romantic relationships, we need to return to what matters most to us, as we discussed in Chapter Two. In the complexity of our relationships, we can never know the 'right answer' ahead of time. All we can do is understand ourselves and what matters to us and act as the most skilful, wisest and noblest version of us we can. By doing that and using the tools and ideas contained in this chapter (and the wealth of amazing ideas available in the world), anyone can improve any relationship. *You can choose* to do that, starting today, by yourself or with your partner. If you do, it will begin to help both you and your partner to grow, heal and learn.

It is important that we hold our boundaries in our relationships as much as anywhere else in our lives and relationships sometimes come to an end. When we have the choice available to us, about whether to hold our boundaries with someone or about whether to start or end a relationship, the assumption *what if everyone is doing their best?* can guide us out of judgment and the sense of what should be in our relationship and into a sense of how things actually are.

It might show us, for instance, that in a particular relationship, we are not able to love ourselves *and* our partner, using Scott Peck's definition, by staying in the relationship. In relationships with people with destructive tendencies, for example, you may notice that to extend yourself for their growth, you are in some way holding yourself back from your own growth. You may notice that, if someone is unable to hold to their commitment of love as Scott Peck defines it, then you need to leave them behind to truly extend yourself for your or their growth. When we see these things clearly and with a commitment to Scott Peck's definition of love, we can take more decisions as our Higher Selves and be as sure as we can that we are doing things for the best and that we are not making things worse. We might ask, if I act purely from love, what do I do?

In my life, with the tools I have learned, my previous relationships could have been incredibly different. I wish I could have been more skilful, more my Higher Self, and so, at the least, done a little better and perhaps left people I cared about with fewer relationship scars to take into the rest of their lives. It is even possible that, with the ideas in this book and elsewhere, certain past relationships could have survived and even been as happy as my marriage. In my story, though, the involuntary stop of the break-up and the gifts that came from it, no matter how painful, opened up deep possibilities for me, in my life and in future relationships. These possibilities enabled me to grow as a person and create (in partnership with my wife) something far more special than I have ever been part of before.

The Relationship Imperative

If two people are committed to loving each other in the way that Scott Peck describes, almost anything is possible in a relationship. Creating the most positive, empowering and possibility-filled relationships we can is vital not just to each of us, but to the world.

Our childhood experiences are fundamental to how each of us develop. We learn so much from how our parents are, how they relate to each other and what they do in the world. Children learn not just from what parents say, but from who their parents are and what they do. Even as our parents did their absolute best to give us the best lives they could, our childhoods leave us with the scars and patterns that are at the heart of our greatest struggles and our deepest desires. Sometimes these scars and patterns were passed down to them from their parents and from theirs before that. We will one day (if we haven't already) be passing our own scars, struggles, patterns and wounds onto our own children, even as we are doing everything in our power to give them the best lives we can.

Our romantic relationships have the power to heal and open some of the deepest and most difficult parts of ourselves. They provide an incredible opportunity to understand and heal our traumas and scars. They provide an incredible opportunity to be supported and to receive energy as we do our work in the world to use our strengths and make our contribution.

With each generation, heroic parents work impossibly hard and with all the love they can manage to lessen the burden their children carry. What if we could do even more than that? By changing how we relate to ourselves, to our scars and to our romantic partners, we can heal ourselves and help our partners do the same. We can create a relationship between two people's Higher Selves, which enables each of them to live more wisely, skilfully and nobly. We can break lineages and patterns that may go back generations. We can empower future generations to bring up even more skilful, wiser and nobler children with more access to *their* Higher Selves. Children learn about how to relate and how to be from those around them. It is up to each of us, especially to parents, but also to uncles, aunts, grandparents, godparents and friends, to be the best role models we can be, to be the people we would like children to learn from, even if we don't have children of our own. By changing our relationships and changing ourselves, we can allow the children of the future to flourish.

That is a powerful imperative for us to change our relationships so that together we can change the future.

How Do I Do This?

With the ideas and tools in this chapter and, indeed, this book, I am handing you some keys. They are keys, at the very least, to begin to explore what can happen if you courageously acknowledge that you have much more choice in your relationship than you may think.

Take the ideas and tools and use them. It can feel scary to do this, so start with small experiments. Choose the part of this chapter that feels the most exciting or the most interesting or the safest – it doesn't really matter which part – and then experiment with it, in a small way, where the risk is lowest. See what happens for your partner as you lean across the divide. Or experiment with scoring some points: do some small things for her or appreciate him when you really feel it inside you. Notice what happens.

Share something from this chapter with your partner. Maybe they are ready and you are, too, to make a commitment to Scott Peck's definition of love. Maybe they will find a story or an idea from this chapter interesting. Share it with them: 'I read this interesting thing about how men think. What do you make of it?' or 'I read this guy writing about how women's and men's awareness is different. Is this really what it's like for you?' Whether the idea resonates with them or not, these conversations will open something up: the ability to talk about your differences and understand each other more. This greater understanding will make it easier to get out of judgment and to see things more as they are by assuming that your partner is doing their best. You will create a space where the two of you can look at the relationship. From there, you can grow it: expanding it to include what it was before and what you can now see together.

Lastly, if you're anything like me, then your romantic relationships may be one of the places you find yourself most triggered in your life. Remember that you may have (subconsciously) selected your partner because of the way that they push your buttons. Remember, too, that because of this, they are uniquely suited to helping you heal. Each time you find yourself triggered, remember that *curiosity is the antidote to contraction*. Each contraction is an opportunity to heal some of the deepest and most ingrained patterns of your life. Look deeply: look at yourself, your previous relationships and those of your partner. Look at the lineage of relationships of your family and that of your partner. Get curious: what is really going on here? What if it's not about the chicken (Chapter 3), it's about the patterns passed down through generations?

Above all, remember that you can choose your adventure, inside and out: *you can choose* to see your partner in a different way, as though they are doing their best, acknowledging the differences and the similarities. *You can choose* to see love as extending yourself for your and your partner's spiritual growth. *You can choose* to engage your curiosity each time your partner presses your buttons or triggers your patterns. *You can choose* a relationship where you grow and heal and support your partner to grow and heal, even whilst acknowledging the flaws and struggles you face.

My hypothesis is that, as you do this, you will spend less and less time contracted and be more and more fulfilled. You will be able to see the truth far more easily and you will learn so much about your Deeper Self, about the unconscious patterns that often run your life. You will be able to act in your relationship more as your Higher Self. You will be able to love your partner more purely as they are, for all they have and all they do not. And through this love and support you will see a transformation in your life as you move out into the world, more secure, less fearful and more creative. You will be bolder, braver and more willing to try and fail because you will know more deeply that you are whole and complete: you are human, as imperfect as all of us, but enough. None of us gets it right all the time, least of all in our relationships, but I hope I have shown you over this chapter that *you can choose* to step into your relationship as something in which you can be more skilful, something you can grow and improve.

I am not perfect, and the arguments, fights and failures in my relationship with Emma are still many, but I am getting wiser and more skilful and, indeed, we are getting wiser and more skilful every time we lean into love. Sometimes we fail, but when you know you are on a journey together, a journey of love, then failure does not hold the same fear.

CHAPTER FIVE SUMMARY

Key ideas: Romantic relationships hold a unique place in our life, giving us unparalleled opportunities to heal our scars and be filled up with the love we need to fulfil our potential. Furthermore, available to us today are ideas, insights and tools that can help us navigate our romantic relationships, including break-ups and divorces, without creating new scars for ourselves and our partners.

This is important for us: to support us to live fulfilled lives and to step out into the world with courage and conviction. It is important because the quality of the relationships of the adults around us affects us all deeply when we are growing up. If we can improve the quality of all our romantic relationships, we can give the next generation an even more secure platform on which to live happy, fulfilled lives and to spend more and more time as their Higher Selves.

Two keys to help us to change our relationships into *relationships of possibility* are, first, to choose a particular definition of love and, second, to remember our differences, particularly the differences between men and women. These keys can enable us to assume that our partners are doing their best, to learn more about our Deeper Selves and to live more and more as our Higher Selves.

The ways we are different include the different ways that men and women score points in relationships and the different types of awareness between men and women. The key definition of love comes from M. Scott Peck:

> "I define love thus: The will to extend one's self for the purpose of nurturing one's own or another's spiritual growth."

Exercises, practices and questions for reflection:

- Ask yourself, in your relationships: **in this moment, how can I extend myself to nurture the spiritual growth of myself or another?** Or, in other words, how can I act from love in this moment?

- Say **'I'm sorry.'** Use this or phrases like it to extend yourself across the divide between you and your partner at difficult times, reminding yourself that you are doing it out of love. If you find this difficult, remember that you are sorry that your partner is experiencing pain and that the two of you are not in connection. Remember that you are sorry for any part that you have played in that, consciously or otherwise.

- When you find yourself contracting in your relationship, ask: **what if this person is expressing their love, but I just haven't felt it?** Perhaps this is because different people need different things from their partner in order to feel loved. Ask yourself: how can I do something small that the woman in my life will appreciate? Or: how can I appreciate the man in my life for who he is when I really feel it?

- When you feel yourself becoming disconnected in a conversation with your partner, pause and ask yourself: **what if their behaviour isn't about me?** What if your partner doesn't know that what they are doing is upsetting you because they see the world so differently? Or what if they are judging you because they don't know *you* see the world differently? For instance, what if their attention just works in a really different way to yours?

- **Look at your patterns in your romantic relationships** and the patterns and relationship experiences of your parents or caregivers. Where do the patterns overlap? Where are they surprisingly, sometimes extraordinarily, similar? Then get curious: what's *really* happening?

- *We can choose* to believe that **only by bringing ourselves face-to-face with someone who is able to trigger and activate our old learned hurts and patterns can we learn to heal ourselves.** Similarly, only by our partner coming face-to-face with us, the person who is able to trigger and activate their old learned hurts and patterns, can they learn to heal themselves.

- In moments where you are questioning your relationship, remind yourself of your commitment to extending yourself for the purpose of nurturing your own or another's spiritual growth. Ask yourself: **if I act purely from love, what do I do?**

Further Reading and Learning

- *Moving on: Breaking Up without Breaking Down* by Suzie Hayman

- *The Road Less Travelled* by M. Scott Peck

- *The War of Art* by Steven Pressfield

- *Men Are from Mars, Women Are from Venus* by John Gray

- *Beyond Mars and Venus* by John Gray

The Power to Choose: Finding Calm and Connection in a Complex World

- *The Amazing Development of Men (2nd Edition)* by Alison Armstrong

- *Understanding Women* by Alison Armstrong

- *Getting the Love You Want* by Harville Hendrix

CONCLUSION

My life is so different now to how it was when an involuntary stop began to show me that I could look at the world differently. I hope that, through this book, you have seen new possibilities, too. I hope you have had ideas and insights sparked about yourself, your career and your relationships. Above all, I hope you are spending less of your time wrapped up in the patterns and coping mechanisms that are buried in your Deeper Self. I hope, instead, that you are stepping forth into the world clearer, crisper and more skilful, using more of your potential, your Higher Self.

The Freedom to Choose One's Own Way

Recently, in a training course I took part in, someone shared these words, from Austrian psychiatrist and Holocaust survivor, Viktor Frankl: "Everything can be taken from a man but one thing: the last of the human freedoms – to choose one's attitude in any given set of circumstances, to choose one's own way." When I read Frankl's words, I was deeply touched. Who could speak with more authority on that than someone who went through the concentration camps? What Frankl says, of course, is that *you can choose*. Hold that with you, as you go: catch yourself furious in a slow queue at the coffee shop or anxious before a presentation and remind yourself that *you can choose* something different.

This isn't always easy to do. Jordan Hall, the futurist I mentioned back in the introduction, refers to living as your Higher Self as being sovereign. Speaking about how to be sovereign, he first warns us to make sure we are eating well, that we are hydrated, that we are sleeping well. Look after yourself physically as you go on this journey. Next, he says we need to look at our trauma. If we want to interact with others at our most skilful and be as sure as possible that we are making things better and not worse, we need at least to be aware of the things that may trigger us, the contractions we may have. If you bring *curiosity is the antidote to contraction* with you on your journey, then every time you find yourself contracting becomes an opportunity to learn something more about your Deeper Self, the values, patterns and instincts that sometimes rule your behaviour. Once we can see them, by using our curiosity, we can step away from them and *we can choose*. Remember, these big feelings aren't about what they seem. They aren't about the chicken. They aren't about the suits.

The Challenge to You

As part of the introduction to this book, I included a call to arms. In essence, in the face of an uncertain world and an uncertain future, we must each make sure we are doing all we can. That means showing up in the world and doing good work, in both meanings of the word 'good': doing work skilfully and well, yes, but also doing noble work, which is for the greater good. This means being trapped less often by having a mind that evolved for simpler times. It means becoming fitter for complexity. It means using every opportunity, from our careers to our romantic relationships and beyond, to learn about the deeper parts of ourselves and to take leadership in our lives by choosing to live from our Higher Selves whenever we can.

Conclusion

In your work, beware false assumptions of competition: they keep us from doing our best work. Choose to build your success and compete, where competition is genuinely necessary, on the things that you do uniquely well. No one can compete with you at being you. Understanding and then using all the gifts you have is a sure-fire way of ensuring that you are having the greatest positive impact you can. Each time I remember this and choose to be more *me*, rather than trying to be more someone else, I not only feel better, but I find my work and results improve. After all, what is my Higher Self but the clearest, purest version of me, released into the world skilfully, freed from fears and contractions and triggers?

In the complex world we live in, we are more connected to other people than ever before and so many of the challenges we face are in interpersonal relationships. That is why the assumption *what if everyone is doing their best?* is so useful in our everyday lives. Our assumptions about others are so often too simple: flawed and leading to unnecessary conflict and tension. Nowhere, perhaps, is this truer than in our romantic relationships, especially where the differences between men and women are concerned. But it's OK that it's hard: the hardships are one of the greatest gifts of our relationships. Remember, after all, Harville Hendrix's idea that we select our partners because they are uniquely suited to cause contractions in us and therefore – if we remember that *curiosity is the antidote to contraction* – they give us the opportunity to move past our deepest scars: only together can two people as flawed as you and I heal.

The truth is that it has been several years now since I last put concerted energy into learning more about how to be skilled in romantic relationships, but that doesn't stop my learning and healing because I am regularly reminded in my relationship how the principles and ideas in Chapter Five of this book must be practised and refined over and over and over again. Above all, this is done by remembering the words of M. Scott Peck: "I define love thus: The will to extend one's self for the purpose of nurturing one's own or another's spiritual growth."

When Things Change for the Better

It's up to you now.

It's up to you to understand your Deeper Self, using curiosity to understand all the instincts and patterns that sometimes leave you trapped or lead to you acting as your smaller, pettier self. You have the power to choose. Choose to live more from your Higher Self, choose to be the most skilful, wisest, noblest version of you that you can be. When you step out into the world more and more as your Higher Self, you can create more impact in your work and be sure that you are making your impact in the best way possible. You can pursue honourable, noble aims. You can create more connected relationships and be sure that each interaction is sending ripples of possibility out into the world. You can be sure that you are adding to the spirit of the world, not draining it.

If you find yourself adrift in the storms of complexity in today's world, wrapped in stress and anxiety, and feeling, as the developmental theorist, Robert Kegan, might put it, 'in over your head,' this might all feel lofty and far away. That's OK. That's part of this. It might not happen overnight, but by taking greater perspective on the things that are happening to you, you can grow your ability to navigate the storms, until one day you may get your head above the surface of the water and stay there. You do this by remembering that *you can choose* to see things in new ways, with ever more nuanced perspectives, and choosing to do that over and over again.

The ideas in this book can take us from a world 'happening to me' to a world 'created by me' and beyond, from a sense of being stuck and paralysed to creative, inspired action. Then, anything can happen. We can start a business, find a loved one, heal a friendship. We can leave a job, ask the person we love to marry us or even write a book.

The principles in this book won't instantly make any of that easy. This is a journey of growth and discovery, not a destination. It offers a series of steps for developing a set of mental muscles. There will almost certainly be days, as there are for me, where you find yourself trapped in your head, victim to your thoughts and circumstances, but gradually, those times will become fewer and farther between and they will pass quicker. You will notice that the 'you' of today is more curious, more creative, more resilient and more loving than the 'you' of yesterday.

You may find that you are less stressed and that your relationships are stronger, more resilient and more full of possibility than before. I hope all of that and more will allow you to thrive in the face of the complexity of the 21st century.

The ideas in this book won't always be easy to follow, but they will offer you something to turn to in the moments when you struggle. They offer you the next small step in the direction of your Higher Self.

If you choose to take the next step, and then the next, and then the next…well, that's when things get interesting. That is when things change for the better: when we remember that we have the power to choose.

ACKNOWLEDGMENTS

So many people have worked on this book.

Steve Creek was the first editor to work on it with me, as he has been on so much of my writing over the years. He helped nudge it forward when it might otherwise have stalled.

Lily Khambata was the editor who guided it and me from something really quite messy to what you now read.

Scott Mason was the final editor, who helped smooth it into this final draft.

Stefan at Spiffing Books and Megan at Sheer Design and Typesetting did amazing jobs on the cover and layout respectively.

Alex Swallow was a tireless test reader of a very early draft, whose questions and promptings turned it from a 20,000-word essay into an 80,000-word behemoth (which I then cut down).

Other people who generously gave their time to read, proof, feedback and much more were Faisal Sheikh, Katarina Lezova, Colin Smith, Susana Goncalves, Ewan Townhead, Pete Armstrong, Mary Swale and Emma Swale. If you gave feedback on this book and I haven't listed you here…I'm so sorry! That's part of what happens if you take years to get a book out. Please let me know so I can update this section in a future edition.

On the publishing journey, huge thanks to Joni Zwart, who gave invaluable feedback and also put her reputation on the line to connect me to publishers. And thanks to the publisher who gave me an offer to publish this book – I didn't take you up on it, but you helped me believe.

Huge thanks to the many people who have helped me engage my curiosity, particularly as the antidote to my contractions. That includes Joel Monk, Katie Harvey, Mike Toller, Rich Litvin, Robert Holden, Myles Downey, Graham Johnston, Julia Dvinskaya and more.

Thank you to everyone who worked on the *12-Minute Method* books: they were a necessary step to attempting to finally finish and then publish this one. They were the (huge) small steps that made me capable of getting here.

All the clients who have worked with me over the years, especially the ones who let me share their stories, have changed who I am and informed this book. If you'd like to do one-to-one work with me on the kinds of ideas outlined here, or in the context of a complex leadership role, email hello@robbieswale.com.

When I do my work on what my strengths are, one of them is about collecting inputs that can be shared with others at the perfect time. This book and my work would be so much poorer without the shoulders of the amazing giants on which it all stands. I've named them throughout, but particularly those who contributed most to the core ideas of each chapter in Part One: the Zanders, Brené Brown, Guy Sengstock. You mostly don't know how much your work has affected my life, but it has.

Acknowledgements

When I do work to understand what my unique ability might be, what my Zone of Genius is, here's the kind of thing that comes: sharing myself, deeply and with love, with others. I have to say that, in the past few months, I've found myself asking: is that even a valid way to write a book?

But who cares? It's me competing based on *my* strengths. Thanks for being here to read it.

HELP SPREAD THE WORD

The ideas in this book can have an incredible impact on someone's experience of life. In the stress-filled complexity of the modern world, this has never been more important.

If you can, please help spread the word in one or both of these ways:

Leave a Review on Amazon

It really can't be overstated how important reviews are to help a book reach the people it's intended to help. If you have taken something positive from reading this book, please spare five minutes of your time to help someone else find their something positive, too. You never know where it might take them.

Even just a rating and one sentence will make a big difference. You can do that here:

http://geni.us/powertochoose

Tell Someone About This Book

Who is the person in your life for whom these ideas could have the biggest impact? Take a few minutes now to reach out and let them know.

It'll make a difference for me, but most importantly it could make all the difference for them, on their stress, their relationships, and their impact on the world.

FREE eBook:
A Condensed Summary of This Book

This is a book full of practices.

The thing about practices is you have to practise them.

To help you do that, I want to share with you a condensed pdf summary of this book.

It contains all the chapter summaries from this book in one place: the key ideas, actions, practices and references from the book condensed into nine pages.

To get this free gift (and an Action Sheet designed to help you record and take action on your insights) visit www.robbieswale.com/power-to-choose-gifts or scan the QR code below.

WHAT TO READ NEXT

The 12-Minute Method Series

How to Start (a book, business or creative project) When You're Stuck

How to Keep Going (with a book, business or creative project) When You Want to Give Up

How to Create the Conditions for Great Work

How to Share What You've Made

Available from Amazon, here, or from your favourite bookshop:

Other Notable Works

The Meaningful Productivity Blueprint – available for free at www.robbieswale.com

An Introduction to The Coaching Business Flywheel – available for free at www.thecoachsjourney.com

ENDNOTES

Introduction

1. You will notice throughout the book that I write about things that have changed for me as happening 'more than before' or 'less than before' and almost never anything as certain as 'all of the time.' This is a journey; it is about progress, not something that has or will become 'complete.' Whenever I start to think of myself as 'complete,' I notice that life has a habit of smacking me in the face.
2. For more of my thinking on complexity-fit ways to relate to time, download The Meaningful Productivity Blueprint at www.robbieswale.com/meaningful-productivity

Chapter One

1. Choose Your Own Adventure® is a registered trademark of Chooseco LLC.
2. For more on this, see my 12-Minute Method books, starting with *How to Start When You're Stuck*.
3. As a reminder, when I tell a story about a client in this book, details have been changed to preserve the confidentiality of the client. Sometimes several clients' experiences have been amalgamated and sometimes I have asked permission from the client and they have kindly given it. In each case, this is done to maintain the spirit of the experience whilst preserving the vital confidentiality in my work.
4. It's believed that this puzzle is where the phrase 'thinking outside of the box' comes from! You can find a solution to it in the summary at the end of this chapter.

5   My Wife and My Mother-in-Law' (1915), illustration by William Ely Hill. Public domain image via Wikimedia Commons.
6   I'll touch more on the positive sides of competition in Chapter Four.
7   The seed of doubt that can result from questions like this is vital in shifting from fixed perspectives and opening ourselves to new possibilities. We will come back to questions like this over the course of this book.
8   This article from Which? suggests the average size of houses built in the UK since 2010 is 67.8m2 (www.which.co.uk/news/2018/04/shrinking-homes-the-average-british-house-20-smaller-than-in-1970s/). Rounding that up to 75m2 and then multiplying by 8.22billion (estimated 2025 population) gives us an area of 616,500km2. The area of Texas is 696,200km2.
9   The Food and Agriculture Organisation of the United Nations, for example, declared that in 2015 there were 200 million fewer undernourished people than there were in 1990, despite the population increasing by more than 2 billion people in that time (www.nytimes.com/2015/05/28/world/united-nations-reports-global-hunger-down-since-1990.html). Although data seems to show a slight increase in the proportion of undernourished people in the world between 2015 (7.7%) and 2023 (9.1%), total population has increased by so much that there are still more 'not undernourished' people in 2023 than there were in 2015. Data on this and much more is available on the amazing website www.ourworldindata.org. None of this means, of course, that we don't need to continue to do important work to support the poorest people in the world to have enough to eat.
10 This categorisation is, of course, invented and what is present in any moment could be split in other ways. These categories, though, seem to be a particularly useful split for this exercise.
11 Steven Covey, author of *The 7 Habits of Highly Effective People*, used this phrase in his work. He expands: "We see the world, not as it is, but as we are – or, as we are conditioned to see it. When we open our mouths to describe what we see, we in effect describe ourselves, our perceptions, our paradigms."

12 It's worth noting that many coaches and psychotherapists believe that lasting change can only happen when deep embodied work is included, not with work on our thoughts alone. We'll touch on this a little in Chapter Three when we discuss the work of Peter Levine and polyvagal theory. I have felt and seen the value of embodied work, but I have also been part of transformation that appears to come simply from retelling our stories and then taking these retold stories out into our lives.

Chapter Two

1 See Chapter One.
2 This is an adaptation of Hanlon's razor, an aphorism that, according to Wikipedia, is probably named after Robert J Hanlon, who once submitted it to a jokebook. Hanlon's razor is: 'Never attribute to malice that which is adequately explained by stupidity.'
3 You might find that when you choose to assume that someone is doing their best (or is acting with incompetence and not malice), you begin to see evidence to support this assumption, evidence that you didn't notice before. This is because parts of our brain filter what we notice in the world based on what we believe is important: this is why when we are learning to drive, we notice more L plates and when we are preparing to move house, we notice more 'To Let' and 'For Sale' signs. There aren't more L plates or signs, it's simply that our brain shows us more of them. As I discussed in Chapter One, what we see isn't everything that is there. Sometimes changing our assumptions can have a significant impact on what we notice as we go about our lives.
4 Some of this section is quoted directly from *Rising Strong*, to ensure I'm telling it exactly as Brown does rather than from the vagaries of my memory.
5 Even for those readers who aren't familiar with the intricacies of the UK railway network, I imagine you will be able to draw a parallel here with something else you have experienced when 'the rules' of a situation or institution seemed unjustly set against you.

6 On some level, the train guard may have already been making an assumption about us at this point: perhaps something like 'these people are trying their luck because the train is full and they don't want to stand.'
7 *Difficult Conversations with Fred Kofman* from Lean In: www.youtube.com/watch?v=_TNrSo1brdY
8 It is not hard to find empathy for the train guard in retrospect. I imagine that making sure only people with First Class tickets sit in First Class is one of the most difficult parts of a guard's job, often leading to confrontation, and it may be one of the bits he is judged on most harshly by his superiors. He also needs to look after and be fair to the First Class passengers who have paid extra to be in a quieter and more spacious carriage. Not only that, but in the story in question, the guard had probably just worked his way through the whole train, full of frustrated people, hot and crowded, annoyed and frustrated that reservations weren't where they were supposed to be.
9 Essentially, fight/flight/freeze is the idea that when under threat, our brains and bodies tend to respond in one of those three defensive ways: fight the danger, flee from it or freeze and hope not to be noticed. These responses happen incredibly quickly and without the awareness of our rational mind. I'll describe more about what might be happening – moving out of one of those defensive states and into a social engagement state – when I introduce some parts of the neuroscience of Polyvagal Theory in Chapter Three. It is, of course, a little more nuanced than we might instantly assume, for example, it should also be noted that this idea is often now expanded to include the 'fawn' response.
10 Reproduced with permission from *Follow the Lady with the Pink Parasol along the Winding Path* by Pete Armstrong.
11 As in the story of the train guard, however, 'confrontation' from our Higher Selves usually has a very different flavour to confrontation from our baser instincts.

Chapter Three

1. Whilst being triggered might bring any historical experience into the present, it is used almost exclusively to refer to difficult experiences.
2. The quotations from Porges and Levine in this section come from that Rebel Wisdom series, the first part of which is available at www.youtube.com/watch?v=EUNHj5eh7BM
3. I was working on a draft of this book at the time I had this conversation with the psychotherapist and I have to say I almost laughed at him seeming to quote back to me one of the key principles of the book (which he, of course, hadn't read). As one of my coaches is fond of saying, we teach what we most need to know.
4. The inverted commas are here to remind us that *we can choose* to believe that the people and things we see aren't really triggering us: our response is what counts.
5. The quotes from Levine and story about Jamie Wheal in this section come from the Rebel Wisdom series *The Science and Psychology of Polarisation*. The first video in the series can be found here: www.youtube.com/watch?v=EUNHj5eh7BM
6. Softening the gaze and breathing out with a hum are other things that support our shift out of threat and into the social engagement state. Remember that the vagus nerve connects our face to our organs and nervous system more broadly, so changing the way our face is (by shifting the way our eyes are or vibrating our nose through a hum) affects our physiological and psychological experience.

Chapter Four

1. If you want further practical inspiration on moving forwards with the work that matters most to you and to find more of my thoughts on how to get unstuck and do work that makes an impact, see my *12-Minute Method* series. Read more about them at www.robbieswale.com and get your copies from your bookshop of choice.

2 As I used *curiosity is the antidote to contraction* on my response to terms like 'C-Suite,' I came up with some personal insight. Perhaps, like the story about the suits in Chapter Three, it takes me back to the memory of joining a school aged eight or nine and suddenly being in a place where there were so many rules and terms that I didn't know or understand. I was scared, I got things wrong and I didn't feel I belonged, which is a dangerous feeling for a child and for many early humans: if I don't belong, I might be cast out. Perhaps the other children know because they belong and I don't know because I don't belong. Perhaps this coach knows because he belongs as a coach and I don't know because I don't. By this point, I did actually know what 'C-suite' meant (see the next footnote), otherwise perhaps the trigger would have been even greater, calling me back even more to those frightening childhood or evolutionary moments of not belonging.
3 'C-suite' refers to the group of top-level executives in a company, whose job titles often start with the letter C, such as CEO, CFO and CMO.
4 There are echoes here of the two stories about the Victorian scene that I told in Chapter One. We have to be careful of too much certainty, which may hold us back from seeing the full picture.
5 We can look at the economic systems of many of our countries in this way. There's a strong case that the competition and innovation present in market-driven economies has given us ways to feed far more people than ever before and lifted millions out of poverty. At the same, disasters like the 2013 Rana Plaza garment factory collapse in Bangladesh show what can happen when competition encourages people or companies to cut corners with disastrous consequences.
6 Remember, you're already working on another important component of what the world needs by reading this book: to act more from your Higher Self and, as a result, to be as sure as you can that the work you are doing in the world is making things better and not worse.
7 www.gallupstrengthscenter.com

8 Taking action doesn't have to be big. In fact, it's often best when the steps are as small as possible. Focus on getting moving and building momentum first. For more on how to take action and make it manageable, see my *12-Minute Method* books, particularly *How to Start When You're Stuck*.

Chapter Five

1 It was Pressfield's use of the term 'Higher Self' in *The War of Art* that first caught my imagination and led in the end to it being a core concept in this book.
2 It's probably worth noting that although *Men Are from Mars, Women Are from Venus* was written decades ago, the insights contained in it shouldn't be dismissed lightly. It has transformed the lives of thousands of people, including me.
3 It is remarkable to me, given how long ago *Men Are from Mars, Women Are from Venus* was written, just how much it has made a positive, almost instantaneous difference in my life. This includes Gray's list of ways to score points with a Venusian, almost all of which, I discovered when re-reading it for this book, I have embedded in my way of acting in our relationship and almost all of which seem to make a notable difference.
4 The common figure that many of us hold in mind is that half of all marriages end in divorce. As with many things, it isn't quite as simple as that, as this article on Psychology Today explains: www.psychologytoday.com/gb/blog/heart-the-matter/201704/do-half-all-marriages-really-end-in-divorce.

www.ingramcontent.com/pod-product-compliance
Lightning Source LLC
Chambersburg PA
CBHW020409080526
44584CB00014B/1245